Creative MEAT Cooking

Creative MEAT *Cooking*

MARY NORWAK

ISBN 0 86124 007 3
Printed in Hong Kong

This edition published 1978
by Book Club Associates
by arrangement with
Bison Books Ltd

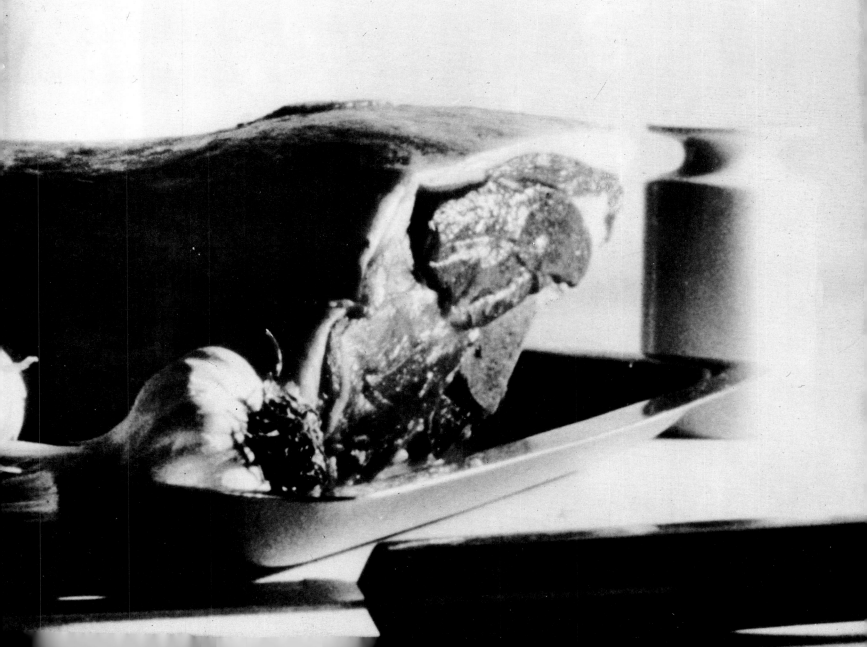

Man was born to be a meat-eating creature. Long before our ancestors had mastered the art of growing grain and vegetables, they were hunters, subsisting on the flesh of what they could trap or hunt. Today we enjoy meat as an essential part of a well-balanced diet and love the variety of flavor and texture which is available to us.

Meat is good for us, with all the necessary mineral elements for good health, phosphorus which combines with calcium to build and maintain strong bones, teeth and nails. Above all, meat is extremely rich in protein which is a body-building material which is broken down into amino acids during the process of digestion. Ten amino acids are considered essential for children, and eight for adults, and all are present in meat. Another essential is iron, present in all meat, and an essential ingredient to keep our blood in good working order.

Some of us may not care too much whether this food is good for us, but in fact it is the protein in meat which gives the mouth-watering scent during cooking and provides the delicious flavor. This savory smell does us good, exciting the flow of gastric juices and preparing our digestive system for the coming meal.

The secret of successful meat cookery and a tasty meal lies in the butcher's shop. A butcher is a craftsman, taking a pride in his raw material and knowing that his reputation depends on careful selection, correct cutting and the subsequent cooking. Meat buying is a two-way business though. The butcher plays his part by selecting well-farmed meat, hanging beef or lamb so that the muscles relax and the meat is tender, and chilling pork or veal. He may prepare and cure his own salted meats or choose them from a good supplier. When the meat reaches the shop, it has to be cut into acceptable pieces and trimmed of excess fat and bone. Then the butcher has to be a friend and advisor to his customers, collaborating with the experienced ones, and carefully guiding those who are uncertain.

The consumer has a part to play too, for while one may rely on a supplier, it is important to choose a piece of meat which is suitable for its purpose and to cook it with care. Even the finest steak can be ruined by careless cooking, and careful timing and the correct temperature for cooking all kinds of meat is important. The clever cook will balance a budget, too, using economy cuts in tasty braises and casseroles and making the best of seasonal vegetables and accompaniments to offset the high cost of quality meat for roasting and grilling (broiling). In this book we aim to simplify the buying and cooking of meat so that everyone can truly enjoy this delicious food.

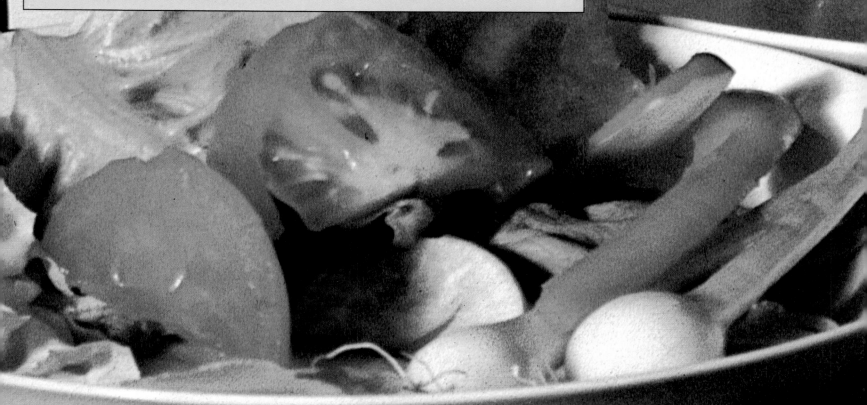

GLOSSARY

American	British
baking/roasting pan	baking/roasting tin
baking soda	bicarbonate of soda
broil	grill
blender	liquidizer
canned	tinned
cheesecloth	muslin
chicory	endive
cornstarch	cornflour
crackers	biscuits
cream, table	single cream
cream, whipping	double cream
dripping	drippings
eggplant	aubergine
endive	chicory
molasses	treacle
mustard, dry	mustard powder
mustard, prepared	made mustard
ovenproof	ovenware
papertowels	kitchen paper
pie shell	pastry case
roast or cut (of meat)	joint
scallions	spring onions
skillet	frying pan
steaming mold	pudding basin
thread	cotton
toothpick	cocktail stick
wax paper	greaseproof paper
whip/beat	whisk
variety meats	offal

Conversions

Comparing conversion units between recipes is not to be encouraged. Each recipe in this book has been individually tested so that the dish will turn out properly. Thus in some recipes 4 fl oz will be 100 ml and in another, 120 ml; however the other measurements of ingredients within the recipe have been adjusted accordingly. Similarly 8 oz of breadcrumbs is $2\frac{1}{4}$ cups; 8 oz of butter or sugar is 1 cup; 8 oz of flour is 2 cups.

Confusing? Pick the type of measurement you like, the one which best suits your kitchen and your utensils, *and stick to it*. If your utensils are metric, use the metric units. If you have measuring cups, then use the relevant quantities. Try to be consistent within each recipe and you will produce delicious, appetizing and attractive dishes.

Most cooking terms in this book are self-explanatory, but this quick-reference guide will speed up cooking.

Baste Spoon or pour fat, pan juices or liquid over the meat when it is roasting in the oven or cooking on or under the grill (broiler). This gives moist meat with good flavor.

Bouquet Garni This consists of a sprig of parsley, sprig of thyme and bay leaf tied together or placed in a small muslin bag. The herbs are added to casseroles or stews and removed before service.

Braising This method is used for cooking meats which are not suitable for roasting, and for chops or thick meat slices. Root vegetables should be browned in a little fat and put into the base of a saucepan or ovenproof dish. The meat is then browned all over in a little fat and placed on the vegetables with about ½ cup/¼ pint/125 ml liquid and a tight-fitting lid. The dish should then be simmered gently or cooked in a low oven. Also known as *Pot-Roasting*.

Casseroling This is similar to *Stewing*, but liquid should only come half-way up the solid ingredients. The container should be covered and cooked in a low oven.

Chine (chop) To cut through the backbone or end bone on ribs or loin so that chops or cutlets may be easily separated for carving.

Frying Cooking meats, low in natural fat, in an open skillet or frying pan. A small amount of fat should be placed in the pan and heated until very hot. Brown meat quickly and then reduce heat and cook uncovered until meat is done.

Grilling/Broiling Cooking meat under very high heat. Meat should be lean and well marbled. Any fat at the edges should be clipped to prevent curling and the meat should be placed about 2–5 inches under the grill/broiler depending on its thickness.

Marinade A flavored liquid which can include red or white wine or wine vinegar or cider, oil, carrots, onion, garlic and a variety of herbs and spices which is poured over meat. The meat is soaked in the liquid and can then be cooked in it, or basted with it, to give flavor and tenderness.

Pot-Roasting See *Braising*.

Roasting Cooking meat uncovered in the oven. In this book, a moderate oven is recommended for roasting all meats to prevent shrinkage.

Simmering Cooking food well below boiling point, so that the liquid only just moves. The temperature is around 185°F/85°C. Fast boiling results in the meat breaking into thick stringy fibers without flavor.

Stewing The meat should be cut into small pieces and coated in seasoned flour, then browned in a little fat or oil (this keeps a good flavor and texture for the meat). Vegetables may be added, and then enough liquid to cover the meat. A stew should be cooked very slowly on top of the stove or in a low oven. See also *Casseroling*.

ROASTS

Clever roasting adds pleasure to a hot meal and tender succulent slices from the cold meat – beef, veal, lamb or pork – are hard to beat for a salad meal. To get perfect cold cuts the meat must be cooked so that it is made tender and remains moist. And to get as many cuts as possible from meat it must be cooked so that it does not shrink. These little tricks will produce a masterpiece of a hot roast and superb cold cuts:

Seasoning Brush the roast with salad oil, rub it liberally with dry mustard and sprinkle with pepper, salt and flour, to get a delicious brown and tender crust.

Stuffing Boned Roasts Meat roasted on the bone has the reputation for being sweetest. Boned roasts of lamb, beef and veal packed with seasoned breadcrumbs extend the meat, making more servings and are also full of rich meaty flavor. The stuffings may be varied in many ways.

Slow Oven Roasting Meat cooked very slowly, fat side up and standing on a rack, has minimum shrinkage and so gives maximum servings. Slow cooking also tenderizes the meat. Temperatures between 325°F/ 170°C/Gas Mark 3 and 350°F/180°C/Gas Mark 4, give the best results. Time for cooking at this temperature varies between 30 and 50 minutes per lb/450 g. Allow 40 to 60 minutes for stuffed roasts. Beef takes the least time and is calculated according to the degree of 'doneness' liked. Lamb should not be overcooked; connoisseurs demand a faint pinkness. Veal and pork should be thoroughly cooked.

Bastes and Glazes of ½ cup/¼ pint/125 ml fruit juice blended with 1 tablespoon each of brown sugar and prepared mustard and a spoonful or two of the pan dripping(s) add a gourmet touch to the roast. Spoon the mixture over the roast twice during the last 30 minutes of cooking. Orange or pineapple juice or cider with mustard makes a delicious glaze for any roast.

Pot Roasting A roast of meat cooking in a heavy-lidded pot on top of the stove is as tender and juicy as any oven roast and is less costly. Any of the less tender, and of course less expensive, cuts of meat may be used. Boned or boneless cuts carve well. Topside rump or round or fresh brisket make excellent pot roasts. Rub the meat with oil and mustard and sprinkle with pepper, salt and flour. Brown the roast all over in hot fat, add a cup or two of water, cover and cook very gently, allowing the same time as for oven-roasting.

Carving After taking the roast out of the oven, stand it for 15–20 minutes; it carves more easily and retains more juices this way. Whether you carve the meat with or across the grain depends on what part of the world you were born in. The best trick for good carving is to have a good and sharp carving knife. Beef can be carved thinly or thickly, depending on your taste; lamb, pork and veal are generally cut thickly.

Accompaniments The extras for the roast have a ritual quality – Yorkshire pudding and mustard with beef, mint sauce or red currant jelly with lamb, orange or apple and mustard with pork and veal.

Piquant Sauce made by whipping 1 tablespoon of prepared mustard with 3 tablespoons red currant jelly and served with any hot roast.

Cream Gravy for veal and lamb. Add milk instead of water to the flour stirred into the pan dripping(s), or add celery or mushroom soup from a can. When seasoning any gravy, remember that the bland meats, lamb and veal, like the tang of mustard as much as beef and pork.

Hot Fruits as a delicious extra. Hot peach slices with freshly baked ham, hot pineapple slices with roast lamb, hot orange slices with roast veal, and little baked red apples with roast beef and roast pork.

STUFFINGS

The most unexpected cuts of meat can be stuffed and baked, and are good hot or cold.

Stuffed Shoulder of Lamb Boning a shoulder is simple with a sharp pointed knife, or a butcher will do it. Use a favorite bread seasoning and stuff the meat like a cushion. Alternatively, open the meat out, spread with stuffing, roll and skewer and tie securely into shape. Pot-roast or cook slowly in the oven at 325°F/170°C/Gas Mark 3, allowing 35–40 minutes per lb/450 g. Baste once or twice.

Stuffed Topside or Round of Beef Use a 1½–2 in/3.75–5 cm thick slice of topside, weighing up to 2 lb/1 kg. Cut a deep pocket in it. Stuff with a favorite bread seasoning. Skewer or sew up like a cushion. Pot- or oven-roast it slowly at 325°F/170°C/Gas Mark 3, allowing 35–40 minutes per lb/450 g.

Stuffed Boned Shoulder of Pork Lightly pack a boned shoulder of pork with bread seasoning. Sage and onion or apple stuffing are old-time favorites. Raisins are good in it too. Sew or skewer into shape. Score the fatty side and roast slowly at 325°F/170°C/Gas Mark 3 for 45 minutes per lb/450 g, basting 2 or 3 times with the pan dripping(s).

Stuffed and Rolled Breast of Veal Have about 3 lb/1.5 kg veal breast boned. Top half of the meat with stuffing and fold the other half over this. Skewer and tie securely into shape. Place on rack in roasting pan and cover with slices of bacon. Roast slowly at 325°F/170°C/Gas Mark 3 allowing 45–50 minutes per lb/450 g.

Bread stuffings are as varied as you like to make them. These facts, however, about stuffings do not vary:

* The stuffing should be moist, but neither wet nor dry.

* If the meat is fatty add little or no fat to the bread seasoning.

* Remember dried herbs have a more powerful flavor than fresh.

* Pack the stuffing loosely for it expands during cooking and takes up juices from the meat.

* Stuff a roast just before cooking – never leaving it stuffed and uncooked overnight.

* Extra stuffing can be baked in a separate pan and this is always popular.

* Before carving stuffed meat let it stand at least 10 minutes after it is removed from the oven as it carves better.

* Use stuffed meats within a day or two of cooking, storing lightly wrapped, in the refrigerator or in a cool *airy* place.

Approximate guide to quantities to make up is ¾ cup/3 oz/75 g of bread stuffing to each lb/450 g meat.

An *easy way to prepare* the bread is to cut slices in small cubes. For a difference the bread can be toasted first or the cubes of bread lightly fried.

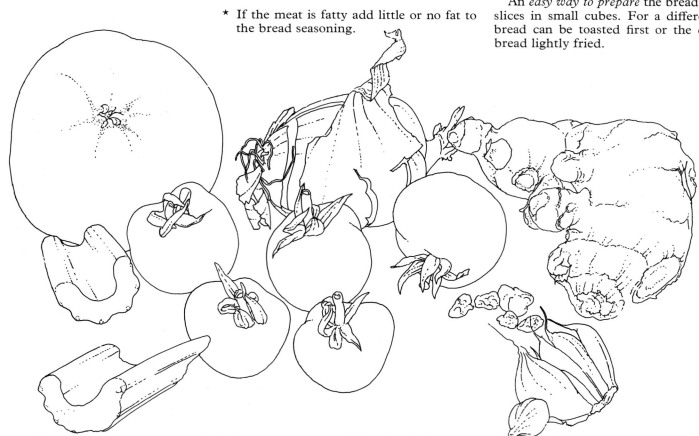

Simple stuffing Use cubes of bread: melt $\frac{1}{4}$ cup/2 oz/50 g butter in a pan. Toss 1 tablespoon or more of finely chopped onion in this. Add 4–6 slices of bread cut in small cubes and stir and toss. Add fresh or dried herbs and other extras to taste. This is a crumbly stuffing; if egg is added it binds the bread more closely.

Basic Crumb Stuffing Mix 6 cups/12 oz/350 g soft white breadcrumbs, $1\frac{1}{2}$ teaspoons dried thyme (or marjoram or mixed herbs), 3 tablespoons chopped parsley, 1 teaspoon grated lemon rind, $\frac{1}{3}$ cup/3 oz/75 g butter or margarine (melted), 3 tablespoons milk (or *lightly* beaten small egg), good sprinkling pepper and salt. This is enough for 4 lb/2 kg meat.

Variations

Sage and Onion Stuffing Use sage instead of thyme. Toss 1 or 2 chopped onions in the butter and add. A leg of lamb stuffed with this is known as, traditionally, 'one legged goose.'

Mushroom Stuffing Omit dried herbs. Toss about $1\frac{1}{4}$ cups/4 oz/100 g sliced mushrooms in the butter and add to the basic mixture. Delicious in roast beef.

Apple Stuffing Peel, core and chop 2 or 3 medium mellow-flavored cooking or dessert apples and add to the basic mixture. A chopped onion, 1 or 2 tablespoons each of chopped celery and seeded raisins go well in an apple stuffing. Excellent for stuffed pork.

Bread and Ham Seasoning Add about 1 cup/4 oz/100 g chopped ham (or boiled bacon) to the breadcrumbs. A finely chopped onion can also be added. This is a good choice for stuffed veal.

Nut and Apricot Stuffing Add 1 heaped tablespoon chopped walnuts and 3 tablespoons chopped dried apricots or dessert prunes to the basic bread mixture. This is delicious for a shoulder of lamb.

Pre-Packaged Stuffings

These are often used for convenience and are made up with hot water and left to stand before stuffing and cooking the roast. Try using hot cider, wine or beer instead of part of the water recommended for making up the stuffing. Extra chopped fresh herbs, nutmeats, dried or fresh fruit can be added to these pre-packaged stuffings. Extra stuffing may be rolled into small balls and cooked around the roast.

Stuffing may also be used to extend chops or steaks if inserted into a pocket cut with a sharp knife in the meat, or can be wrapped in thin slices of meat to be cooked in sauce. Dry pre-packaged stuffing can be mixed with meat for a flavorsome meat loaf, or can be used as a coating instead of plain breadcrumbs for meat or burgers which are to be fried or grilled (broiled).

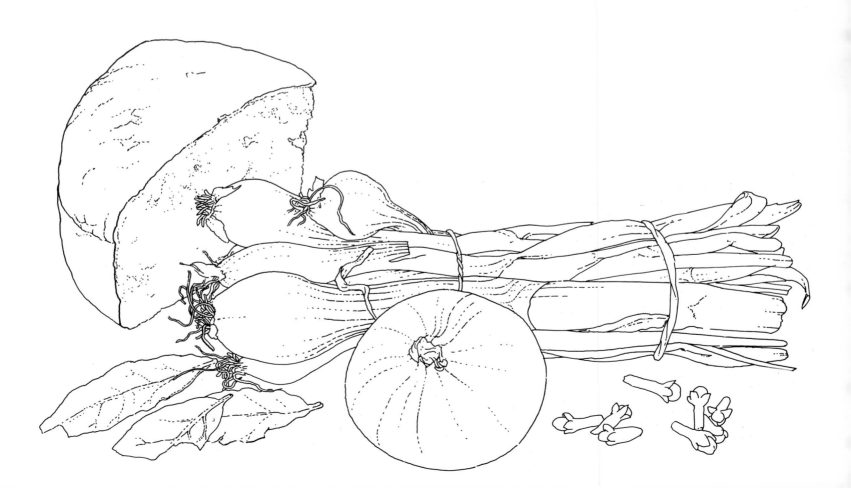

EXTRAS

Roast and grilled (broiled) meats are greatly improved by tasty sauces and other accompaniments. These take little time to prepare but can make all the difference to the flavor and appearance of a meat dish.

Maître d'Hôtel Butter

Soften 2 tablespoons butter (but do not melt). Beat in 1 tablespoon chopped parsley, salt, pepper and a few drops of lemon juice. Form into a small cylinder, chill, and cut into pats to serve on grilled (broiled) chops or steaks.

Mustard Butter

Blend ¼ cup/2 oz/50 g butter with 2 teaspoons of prepared mustard. Form into a small cylinder. Chill and cut into pats to serve on grilled (broiled) steaks or burgers. Sprinkle lightly with paprika.

Steak Tenderizer

Mix 2 teaspoons dry mustard with 2 tablespoons vinegar. Sprinkle over steak and leave in a cool place, but not the refrigerator, for 30 minutes before grilling (broiling).

Golden Basting Sauce

Melt ½ cup/4 oz/100 g butter and fry 1 tablespoon chopped onion until soft and golden. Add 1 tablespoon chopped parsley, 1 tablespoon brown sugar, 2 tablespoons of prepared mild mustard, dash of Cayenne pepper, ½ teaspoon salt and ½ cup/¼ pint stock. Simmer for 5 minutes and spoon over grilled (broiled) chops, steaks or burgers.

Sweet and Hot Mustard Sauce

Mix 4 tablespoons brown sugar, 3 tablespoons dry mustard, good pinch of salt, and 3 tablespoons hot vinegar. Add 1 tablespoon olive oil and a chopped garlic clove. Cover and leave to stand in a cold place for 24 hours. Serve with hot boiled beef, tongue or ham.

Mint Sauce

Cover 4 tablespoons finely chopped fresh mint with 1 tablespoon boiling water. Add sugar to taste, cool and add ½ cup/¼ pint vinegar. Serve with lamb.

Onion Sauce

Chop 2 medium onions, boil until tender and add to 1 cup/½ pint/250 ml well-seasoned white sauce. Serve with lamb.

Caper Sauce

Make up 1 cup/½ pint/250 ml well-seasoned white sauce and add 1 tablespoon capers and 1 teaspoon vinegar. Serve with lamb or mutton.

Cranberry Sauce

Dissolve 3 tablespoons sugar in 5 tablespoons water. Add ¾ cup/4 oz/100 g fresh cranberries and cook gently for 10 minutes. Cool and serve with pork or ham.

Red Currant or Mint Jelly

Serve with hot or cold lamb.

Raisin Sauce

Mix ¼ cup/2 oz/50 g brown sugar, 1 tablespoon cornstarch and a pinch of salt together and mix with 2 tablespoons water. Simmer ¾ cup/4 oz/100 g seedless raisins in 1 cup/½ pint/250 ml water for 5 minutes. Mix raisins and liquid with cornstarch, return to pan and cook until clear and slightly thickened. Stir in 2 tablespoons vinegar and 2 tablespoons butter. Serve with pork or ham.

Cumberland Sauce

Blanch the rind of ½ lemon and the rind of ½ orange in a little water, and cut into very thin strips. Add 3 tablespoons red currant jelly, ½ teaspoon dry mustard, squeeze of lemon juice and ½ cup/¼ pint/125 ml port. Stir over low heat until well blended. Serve with ham or tongue.

Horseradish Sauce

Mix together 6 tablespoons/1½ oz/40 g finely grated horseradish, 4 tablespoons single cream, 1 tablespoon vinegar, 2 teaspoons fine white sugar and a pinch of salt. Serve with beef.

Apple Sauce

Choose cooking apples which cook into 'fluff.' Slice them and cook in just enough water to cover until they form a purée. Sweeten slightly and stir in a little butter. If liked, apples may be cooked in cider. A few raisins may be added just before the apples are cooked. Serve with pork or ham.

Yorkshire Pudding

Sift ½ cup/2 oz/50 g plain (all-purpose) flour and a pinch of salt. Work in 1 egg and ½ cup/¼ pint/125 ml milk, or milk and water. Beat well to a smooth batter and leave to stand. To cook individual puddings, grease an 8-holed baking sheet and heat it in the oven. Pour a little batter in each and bake at 425°F/220°C/Gas Mark 7 for 15 minutes until crisp and golden. The puddings can be cooked while the beef rests before carving.

Dumplings

Mix 1 cup/4 oz/100 g self-raising (self-rising) flour with ½ cup/2 oz/50 g shredded suet and a pinch of salt. Mix to a firm soft dough with cold water and form into 8 small balls. Drop into soups or stews, cover and cook for 20 minutes. If liked, add chopped fresh herbs to dough before cooking.

A ham (or bacon) roast is an invaluable side dish when numbers may unexpectedly increase, or guests' arrival times are uncertain, and it can be a highly decorative affair since a variety of colorful garnishes and glazes can be used. The meat should be weighed, soaked if necessary, then boiled (or roasted) gently, allowing 20 minutes per lb/450 g. The rind should be removed while it is still warm, and the meat put on a rack in a roasting pan before the glaze is used. Roasts should be baked at 400°F/200°C/Gas Mark 6.

Molasses Glaze

Mix 2 tablespoons plain (all-purpose) flour and 2 tablespoons sugar (demerara if available), stir in 2 tablespoons molasses, and mix to a smooth paste with 3 tablespoons warm liquid. Spread the paste over the meat, place in a hot oven and bake for 20–30 minutes until the glaze is crisp and well-browned.

Honey Glaze

Spread 2 tablespoons clear honey over the meat, and sprinkle with 1 tablespoon fine breadcrumbs. Mix $\frac{1}{2}$ cup/$\frac{1}{4}$ pint/125 ml pineapple juice and $\frac{1}{2}$ cup/$\frac{1}{4}$ pint/125 ml vinegar, and pour over the meat. Place in hot oven for 20–30 minutes until golden brown, basting occasionally.

Clove and Sugar Glaze

Score the fat surface of the roast in a crisscross diamond pattern, then stud with cloves. Mix 1 teaspoon ground cloves with 2 tablespoons soft brown sugar. Mix to a smooth paste with ginger ale, spread on the surface, and bake in hot oven for 20–30 minutes until crisp.

Cranberry Glaze

Melt 2 tablespoons cranberry jelly and add 2 tablespoons cider. Spoon over the roast in the pan and sprinkle all over with sugar (demerara if available). Bake in a hot oven for 20–30 minutes until crisp, basting from time to time. Red currant jelly may also be used to make this glaze.

Mustard Glaze

Mix 2 teaspoons French mustard, 2 tablespoons wine vinegar and 2 tablespoons boiling salted water. Pour over the roast in roasting pan. Mix together 2 tablespoons fine breadcrumbs and 1 tablespoon sugar (demerara if available), and sprinkle over the meat. Bake in hot oven for 20–30 minutes until crisp.

Prune and Ginger Glaze

Measure out 1 cup/$\frac{1}{2}$ pint/250 ml prune juice from stewed prunes, and pour over the meat. Mix together 2 cups/2 oz/50 g crushed cornflakes, $\frac{1}{4}$ teaspoon ground ginger and 2 tablespoons brown sugar, and sprinkle all over the roast. Bake in a hot oven until crisp, basting with the juice from time to time.

Sugar and Garlic Glaze

Score the surface fat in a diamond pattern, and put a clove in each intersection. Put 2 halved garlic cloves, 1 cup/$\frac{1}{2}$ pint/250 ml water and 1 tablespoon powdered aspic jelly in a saucepan, and add 2 teaspoons sugar and 2 teaspoons vinegar, and boil until jelly dissolves. Pour over the roast and bake for 15 minutes in hot oven. Baste, remove garlic and bake for another 20 minutes, basting occasionally. Remove from oven, baste again and sprinkle fat with fine breadcrumbs.

Mint Glaze

Score the fat in a diamond pattern and stick a clove in each intersection. Boil 4 large sprigs fresh or dried mint with 1 cup/$\frac{1}{2}$ pint/250 ml water, add $\frac{1}{2}$ package of lemon jelly and allow it to dissolve. Pour mixture over the meat, bake for 15 minutes in hot oven and then baste with liquid. Put more chopped mint around the roast. Bake for another 20 minutes, basting once, then remove from oven and baste again. Pat fine dry breadcrumbs into the fat, then sprinkle with chopped mint.

Pineapple Garnish

Drain canned pineapple rings, sprinkle with sugar (demerara if available), and grill (broil) for a few seconds under a very hot grill (broiler) until the sugar caramelizes. Arrange overlapping rings around the roast, and garnish the top with half-circles of pineapple. Maraschino cherries may be placed in each half-circle.

Glazed Apple Garnish

Peel 8 small apples and remove cores, then fill centers with cream cheese or cottage cheese. Heat a little red currant jelly until just melted, and dip each apple in melted jelly. Bake until just soft, then cool and paint with more melted jelly before serving.

Tomato Garnish

Skin one dozen small tomatoes, cut $\frac{1}{2}$ in/ 1.25 cm from stalk end, and remove a few seeds with a teaspoon. Fill cavities with canned corn, and place in oven until heated through before arranging on dish.

Peach Garnish

Garnish top of roast with sliced canned peaches in a line down center. Place peach halves around dish with a canned cherry in center of hollow of each peach.

Orange Garnish

Slice peeled oranges across the sections. Dip each slice in oil and vinegar dressing. Put two or three slices on top of the meat and arrange remainder around the dish. Sprinkle the orange slices with chopped parsley.

Prune Garnish

Soak prunes several hours in hot water. Drain and remove stones, and fill cavities with ground almonds. Fix each prune on a cocktail stick or toothpick and stand them upright around the roast.

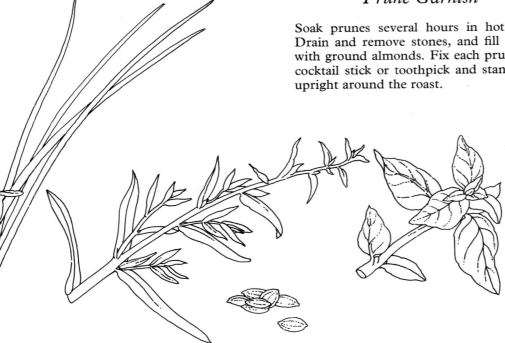

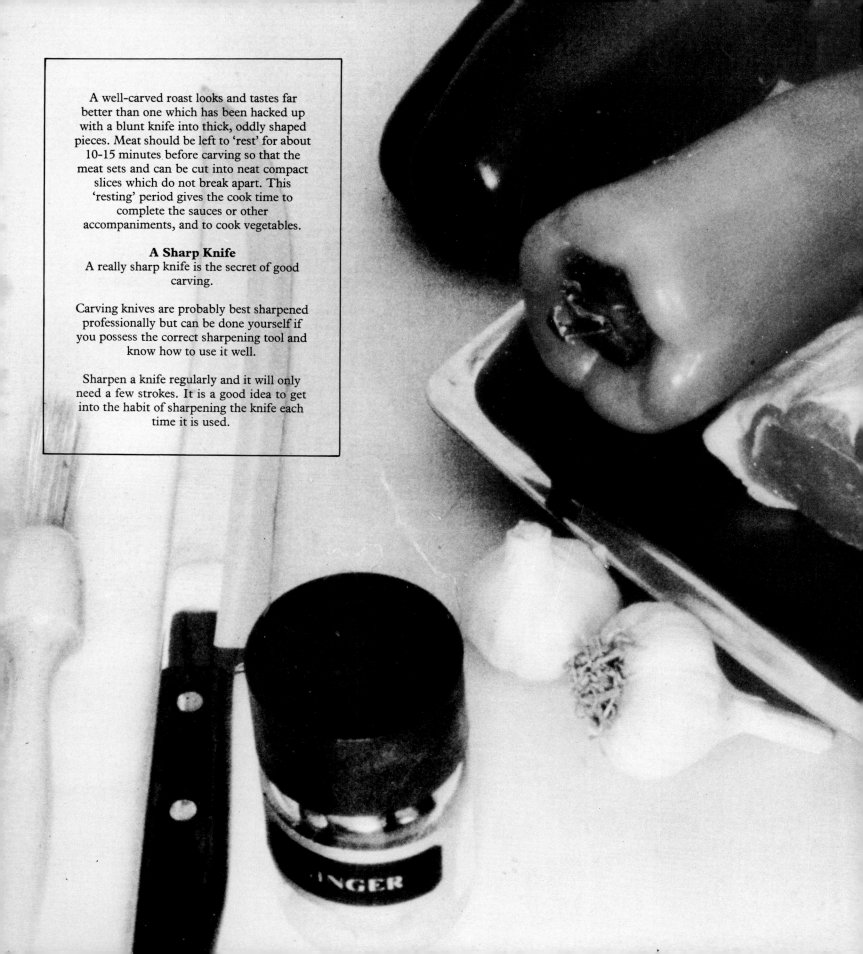

A well-carved roast looks and tastes far better than one which has been hacked up with a blunt knife into thick, oddly shaped pieces. Meat should be left to 'rest' for about 10-15 minutes before carving so that the meat sets and can be cut into neat compact slices which do not break apart. This 'resting' period gives the cook time to complete the sauces or other accompaniments, and to cook vegetables.

A Sharp Knife
A really sharp knife is the secret of good carving.

Carving knives are probably best sharpened professionally but can be done yourself if you possess the correct sharpening tool and know how to use it well.

Sharpen a knife regularly and it will only need a few strokes. It is a good idea to get into the habit of sharpening the knife each time it is used.

BEEF
American Cuts

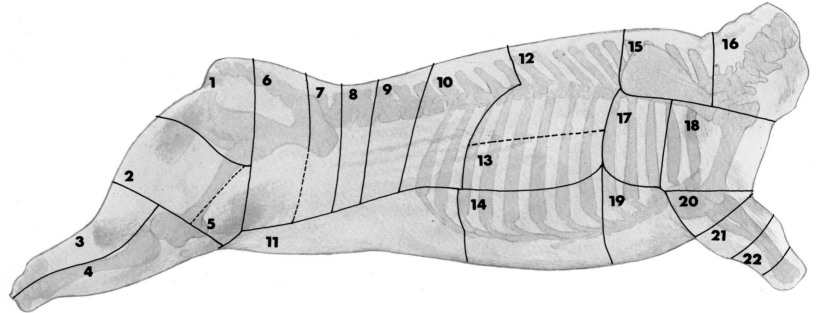

ROUND

1
Rump
Rolled Rump Roast
Rump Steak
Standing Rump Roast
Rump Pot Roast

2
Round
Round Steak
Top Round Steak
Bottom Round Steak (Swiss)
Beef Kebabs

3
Shank
Heel of Round Roast

4
Shank
Hind Shank Roast

5
Round
Tip Steak
Tip Roast

SIRLOIN

6
Sirloin Steak
Tenderloin of Fillet
Sirloin Roast
Beef Kebabs

7
Tenderloin or Fillet
Pin Bone Sirloin Steak
Sirloin Roast
Beef Kebabs

SHORT LOIN

8
Tenderloin of Fillet
Porterhouse Steak
Roast Short Loin

9
Tenderloin or Fillet
Short Loin Roast
T-Bone Steak

10
Club (or Wing) Steak
Short Loin Roast

FLANK

11
Rolled Flank Roast
Flank Stewing Meat
Flank Steak
Flank Fillets

RIB

12
Standing Rib Roast
Rib Steak
Rolled Rib Roast

13
Short Ribs

SHORT END OF BRISKET

14
Short Plate
Rolled Plate Roast
Plate 'Boiling'

CHUCK

15
Chuck
Blade Pot Roast
Blade Steak
Boneless Chuck (Pot Roast)
Triangle Pot Roast

16
Neck
Rolled Neck Roast
Boneless Neck Roast

17
Shoulder
English Cut

18
Shoulder
Rolled Shoulder Pot Roast
Arm Steak

FORESHANK

19
Brisket
Corned Beef
Brisket (Pot Roast)

20
Brisket
Brisket (Pot Roast)

21
Foreshank
Shank Knuckle Roast

22
Foreshank
Cross Cut Foreshank

British Cuts

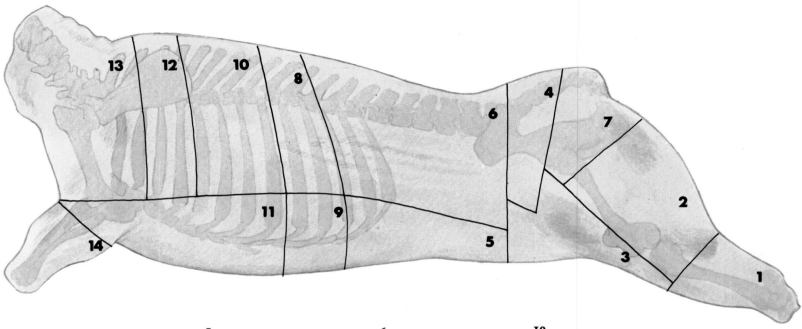

1
Leg
Stewing Meat and meat for soups

2
Round of Beef:
Topside or Silverside
Pot Roast
Spiced or salted Beef
Pot Roast
Boiled Beef

3
Top Rump or Thick Flank
Pot Roast
Stewing Meat

4
Rump
Rump Roast
Chateaubriand
Rump Steak

5
Flank
Flank Pot Roast
Stewing Meat

6
Sirloin
T-Bone Steak
Porterhouse Steak
Sirloin Roast
Sirloin Steak
Wing End of Sirloin Roast
Wing Rib Steaks
Fillet
Fillet Mignon (Tournedo)
Entrecôte Steak

7
Aitchbone
Aitchbone Roast
Salted Aitchbone

8
Forerib
Rib Roast
Boned and rolled Rib Roast

9
Flank
Pot Roast

10
Middle Rib
Back Rib Roast
Top Rib Roast

11
Brisket
Brisket (Pot Roast)
Boned and Rolled Brisket
Slated Brisket

12
Shoulder
Chuck (or Chine) Steak
Blade Steak
Stewing Meat
Leg of Mutton Cut

13
Neck and Clod
Stewing meat

14
Shin
Stewing Meat

Traditional Roast Sirloin

3 lb/1.5 kg boned and rolled sirloin beef
2 tablespoons beef dripping(s)
1 cup/½ pint/250 ml water
Salt and pepper

Heat the dripping(s) and seal the cut surfaces of the meat in very hot dripping(s). Put the meat into a roasting pan and add the cold water. Season and roast at 350°F/180°C/Gas Mark 4 for 20 minutes per lb/450 g and 20 minutes over.

Steak and Mushroom Casserole

1½ lb/675 g chuck or blade steak
¼ cup/2 oz/50 g dripping(s)
4 small onions
1¼ cups/4 oz/100 g button mushrooms
Sprig of parsley
Sprig of thyme
1 bay leaf
1 cup/½ pint/250 ml stock
2 teaspoons cornstarch

Lightly brown the cubed steak in melted dripping(s). Place in a casserole and add quartered onions, mushrooms, herbs and stock. Cover tightly and cook at 350°F/180°C/Gas Mark 4 for 2½ hours.

Beef Casserole with Noodles

Illustrated on pages 44/45

1 lb/450 g chuck or blade steak
2 tablespoons dripping(s)
2 leeks
½ lb/8 oz/225 g tomatoes
Salt and pepper
1½ cups/¾ pint/375 ml dry cider
½ cup/2 oz/50 g Cheddar cheese
1 lb/450 g noodles

Cut the steak in cubes and brown in the hot dripping(s). Lift out the meat and put into a casserole. Cut the leeks in half lengthwise and then cut each half across into two pieces. Cut each piece in half lengthwise: each leek should be divided into 8 pieces. Cook in the dripping(s) until just soft, then drain and add to the meat. Peel the tomatoes but leave them whole. Put with the meat and season well. Pour on the cider, cover and cook at 325°F/170°C/Gas Mark 3 for 1½ hours. Remove the lid and sprinkle the cheese thickly on the meat. Grill until cheese is brown and bubbling. Serve with cooked noodles.

Beef Casserole with Dumplings

1½ lb/675 g stewing steak
¼ lb/100 g ox kidney
1 large onion
12 baby onions
2½ cups/½ lb/225 g carrots
1¼ cups/5 oz/125 g
self-raising (self-rising) flour
1 teaspoon dry mustard
Salt and pepper
¼ cup/2 oz/50 g dripping(s)
1 teaspoon sage
1½ cups/¾ pint/375 ml beef stock
½ cup/1½ oz/40 g shredded suet
Cold water to mix

Cut the steak into 1-in/2.5-cm cubes. Remove the core and cut the kidney into small pieces. Cut the large onion into thin slices. Put 1 tablespoon flour into a bowl with the mustard and add a little salt and pepper. Toss the steak and kidney in the seasoned flour. Melt the dripping(s) in a large saucepan. Fry all the onions and sliced carrots until brown and remove from the saucepan. Fry the steak and kidney in the remaining fat until brown and return the onions to the pan. Add the stock to the pan, bring to the boil and simmer gently for 2 hours. To make the dumplings put the remaining flour and salt into a bowl with the suet and sage. Mix to a firm dough with cold water. Divide into 10 and roll into balls. Drop these on top of the beef stew and cook for a further 15 minutes.

Beef Casserole Provençal

1½ lb / 675 g chuck or blade steak
1 tablespoon olive oil
1 carrot
1 onion
3 tomatoes
1¼ cups / 4 oz / 100 g mushrooms
1 cup / ½ pint / 250 ml stock
12 pitted black olives
1 garlic clove
½ teaspoon salt
¼ teaspoon pepper
Pinch of basil
1 bay leaf

Cut the steak into cubes and brown in hot oil. Lift out meat and put into a casserole. Slice the carrot and onion and cook in the oil until soft. Drain and add to the meat. Add the whole peeled tomatoes, whole mushrooms and stock to the meat. Stir in the olives, crushed garlic, salt, pepper, basil and bay leaf. Cover and cook at 325°F / 170°C / Gas Mark 3 for 2 hours. Remove the bay leaf before serving.

Carbonnade Flamande

2 lb / 1 kg chuck or blade steak
3 tablespoons butter
1 large onion
1 garlic clove
1½ cups / ¾ pint / 375 ml beer
2 teaspoons French mustard
2 teaspoons brown sugar
2 teaspoons malt vinegar
1 teaspoon salt
1 bay leaf
Pinch of thyme
½ cup / 2 oz / 50 g white breadcrumbs

Fry the finely chopped onion and crushed garlic in the butter until golden. Add the cubed beef and fry until brown on all sides. Stir in all remaining ingredients except breadcrumbs. Continue to stir until it comes to the boil. Cover with a tight fitting lid and simmer for 2 hours. Stir in breadcrumbs. Serve with boiled potatoes.

Smothered Beef

Illustrated on pages 40/41

1½ lb / 675 g stewing beef
4 tablespoons oil
2 onions
10½ oz / 298 g can of condensed tomato soup
½ teaspoon celery salt
1 tablespoon prepared mustard
1 tablespoon rosemary
1 teaspoon salt
¼ teaspoon pepper
8 Spanish stuffed green olives

Cut the steak into 8 even-sized pieces. Heat the oil and fry the meat until brown on both sides. Transfer to a casserole. Slice the onions and fry them in the remaining oil for 3 minutes. Add the soup, celery salt, mustard, rosemary, salt and pepper, and bring to the boil. Pour over the meat. Cover with a lid and cook at 325°F / 170°C / Gas Mark 3 for 2 hours. Stir in the sliced olives and serve garnished with a little extra rosemary.

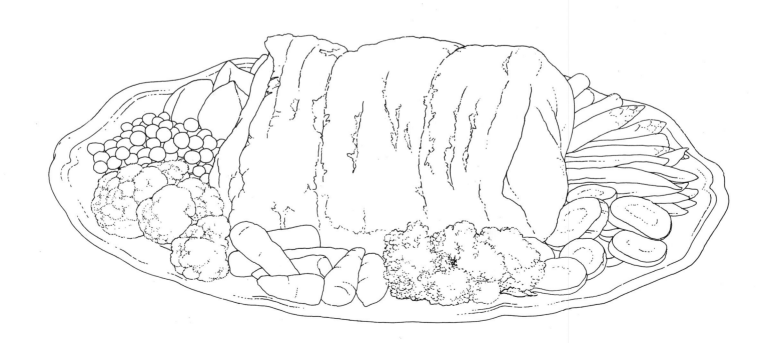

Stir-Fried Beef

Recipe on page 51

Lean beef
Celery sticks
Carrots
Spring onions (scallions)
Oil
Salt and pepper
Spaghetti (or other pasta) in tomato sauce

Boeuf à la Bourguignonne

2 lb / 1 kg chuck or blade steak
$\frac{1}{4}$ cup / 2 oz / 50 g dripping(s)
1 tablespoon plain (all-purpose) flour
1 cup / 8 fl oz / 200 ml red wine
1 cup / 8 fl oz / 200 ml stock
2 garlic cloves
1 tablespoon tomato purée
Salt and pepper
6 slices of bacon (streaky)
20 tiny onions
1$\frac{1}{4}$ cups / 4 oz / 100 g button mushrooms

Cut the meat into 2-in / 5-cm squares. Brown in hot dripping(s). Sprinkle in the flour and brown carefully. Stir in the wine, stock, crushed garlic, tomato purée and seasoning. Cut bacon in small pieces and fry in a separate pan. Add whole onions and cook gently for 5 minutes. Add onions and bacon to meat. Cover with a tight-fitting lid and simmer for 2 hours. Add mushrooms and cook for 10 minutes.

Peppered Braised Beef

2 lb / 1 kg beef top ribs (English cut)
2 tablespoons dripping(s)
1 large carrot
1 large onion
1 teaspoon tomato purée
1 cup / $\frac{1}{2}$ pint / 250 ml stock
Salt and pepper

Sauce
1 tablespoon dripping(s)
1 small green pepper
1 small onion
$\frac{1}{4}$ teaspoon garlic salt
2 teaspoons cornstarch
1 tablespoon water
1 cup / 8 oz / 225 g can of tomatoes

Brown meat in hot dripping(s) in heavy saucepan. Remove meat and fry sliced vegetables for 2 minutes. Replace meat and add tomato purée, stock and seasoning. Cover and simmer for 2 hours. When tender, remove meat and slice. Strain liquid. To make the sauce: heat dripping(s), add the sliced green pepper, onion and garlic salt and cook till tender. Add blended cornstarch to strained liquid, add to sauce and boil for 1 minute. Add sliced tomatoes and pour sauce over meat.

Spiced Herb Steaks

1$\frac{1}{2}$ lb / 675 g
top rump steak (top round steak)
Salt and pepper
2 cups / 4 oz / 100 g white breadcrumbs
2 teaspoons curry powder
$\frac{1}{2}$ teaspoon paprika
2 teaspoons chopped parsley
$\frac{1}{4}$ teaspoon mixed herbs
1 onion
$\frac{1}{4}$ cup / 2 oz / 50 g butter
4 tomatoes

Cut steak into 4 even pieces, season both sides, and place with halved tomatoes in shallow, ovenproof dish. Mix breadcrumbs, curry powder, paprika, parsley, herbs and finely chopped onion. Spread mixture over steaks and dot with butter. Bake uncovered at 350°F / 180°C / Gas Mark 4 for 45 minutes and serve garnished with tomatoes.

Sauerbraten

3 lb/1.5 kg rump of beef
1 cup/½ pint/250 ml water
1 cup/½ pint/250 ml vinegar
5 peppercorns
1 onion
2 carrots
1 bay leaf
¼ cup/2 oz/50 g butter
1 beef cube
1 cup/½ pint/250 ml red wine
3 tablespoons sugar

This dish must be started 3 days before use. Put the beef into a deep dish. Boil water, vinegar, crushed peppercorns, sliced onion, sliced carrots and bay leaf and then simmer for 10 minutes. Leave to cool and then pour over the meat. Cover and leave in a cool place for 3 days, turning the meat often. Drain the meat, reserving the liquid. Melt the butter and brown the meat on all sides. Strain on the vinegar liquid and add the onion and carrot slices to the meat. Stir in the beef cube and wine, and pour over the meat. Bring to the boil, cover and simmer for 2½ hours.

Spring Beef Casserole

Illustrated on pages 36/37

1½ lb/1 kg chuck or blade steak
¼ cup/1 oz/25 g seasoned flour
3 tablespoons oil
2 onions
2 carrots
1 small celeriac (celery root)
14 oz/400 g can of tomatoes
1 cup/½ pint/250 ml beef stock
1 tablespoon Worcestershire sauce
Salt and pepper
Sprig of parsley
Sprig of thyme
1 bay leaf
10 stuffed green olives

Toss cubed meat in seasoned flour. Heat oil in frying pan and fry meat till brown. Put in casserole. Put chopped onions, sliced carrots and cubed celeriac in frying pan and cook till soft. Add to meat in casserole. Mix remaining seasoned flour into oil left in frying pan and brown. Stir in tomatoes. Add to casserole together with stock, Worcestershire sauce, seasoning and herbs. Put on lid and cook at 325°F/170°C/Gas Mark 3 for 2½ hours or until meat is tender. Add halved olives. Check seasoning and remove herbs.

Nine-Day Beef

8 lb/4 kg rump of beef
1 cup/6 oz/175 g dark soft brown sugar
½ cup/3 oz/75 g coarse sea salt
⅔ cup/4 oz/100 g dried juniper berries
2 tablespoons whole black peppercorns
2 tablespoons whole allspice
Pinch of ground cloves
1½ cups/¾ pint/375 ml water
Onions

Rub all sides of meat with the sugar, using the fingertips to work it in. Place the meat in a large covered dish and store in the refrigerator for 2 days. Process salt, juniper berries, peppercorns, allspice and cloves in a blender until finely crushed. For the next 9 days, work 2½ tablespoons of this spice mixture into all sides of the meat each day. On the tenth day, rinse under cold running water. Put into a covered casserole, add the water and bake at 275°F/140°C/Gas Mark 1 for 5 hours until the meat is tender. Remove from the oven, cool and wrap in cooking foil. Put on a weight and refrigerate for 12 hours. To serve, slice thinly, and encircle with very thinly sliced raw onion.

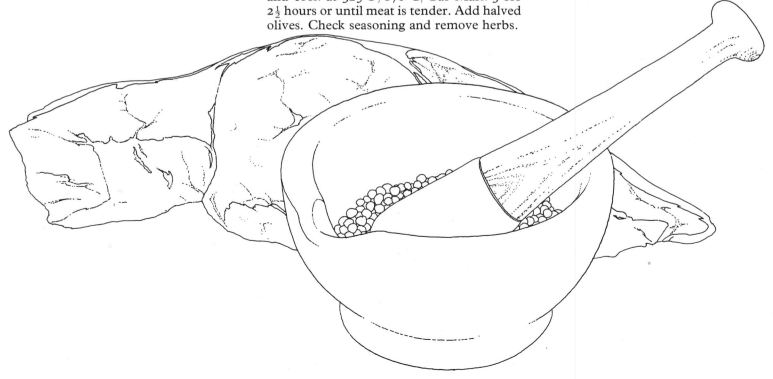

Spanish Country Casserole

Recipe on page 35

Shin or foreshank of beef
Oil
Butter
Carrots
Onion
Garlic
Flour
White wine
Chicken stock
Can of tomatoes
Parsley
Bay leaf
Salt and pepper
Stuffed green olives

Mexican Pot-Roast

3 lb / 1.5 kg top ribs of beef (English cut)
¼ cup / 1 oz / 25 g plain (all-purpose) flour
1 teaspoon chilli powder
1 tablespoon paprika
1 teaspoon salt
¼ cup / 2 oz / 50 g dripping(s)
2 onions
½ cup / ¼ pint / 125 ml water
6 cloves
1 tablespoon cornstarch
2 tablespoons cold water
2 × 15 oz / 425 g cans red kidney beans

Mix the flour, chilli powder, paprika and salt and coat the meat. Brown in hot dripping(s). Put sliced onion in a deep pan, place meat on top, and add water and cloves. Cover and simmer for about 2½ hours until tender. Remove meat and keep hot. Strain liquid and make up to 1 cup / ½ pint / 250 ml with water. Add cornstarch blended with water and simmer for 2 minutes. Serve meat with beans and thickened liquid.

Hunters' Steak

4 thick slices topside beef (top round)
2 carrots
1 onion
1 celery stick
⅓ cup / 3 oz / 75 g butter
¼ cup / 1 oz / 25 g plain (all-purpose) flour
1 cup / ½ pint / 250 ml stock
2 tablespoons tomato purée
½ cup / ¼ pint / 125 ml red wine

Chop the carrots, onion and celery and cook in 2 tablespoons / 1 oz / 25 g butter until golden. Stir in the flour and allow to brown. Add the stock and tomato purée. Bring to the boil and then simmer for 2 minutes. Brown the beef slices in remaining butter and put into an ovenproof dish. Pour on the sauce and cover. Cook at 350°F / 180°C / Gas Mark 4 for 1½ hours. Just before serving, stir in the wine.

Jellied Beef

4 lb / 2 kg brisket beef
12 slices of lean bacon
Salt and pepper
2 cups / 1 pint / 500 ml red wine
¼ cup / 2 fl oz / 50 ml oil
¼ cup / 2 oz / 50 g butter
1 cup / ½ pint / 250 ml stock
Pinch of ground nutmeg
Sprig of parsley
Sprig of thyme
1 bay leaf
4 onions
4 carrots
1 calf's foot

Trim surplus fat from the meat and tie it firmly into a roll. Chop the bacon. Put meat and bacon into a deep dish, season with salt and pepper, and pour on the wine. Leave to soak for 2 hours. Drain the meat and brown it all over in the oil and butter. Put into a casserole with wine and bacon, stock, nutmeg, herbs, sliced onions and carrots, and split calf's foot. Cover and cook at 325°F / 170°C / Gas Mark 3 for 3 hours. Cool slightly and slice beef. Put beef slices into a shallow dish and surround with pieces of vegetables. Strain cooking liquid, cool and pour over meat and vegetables. Leave in the refrigerator until chilled and set.

Boiled Beef and Carrots

3 lb / 1.5 kg rolled salted brisket beef
(in US this is called corned beef)
2 medium onions
3 carrots
12 peppercorns
Sprig of parsley
Sprig of thyme
1 bay leaf

Soak the meat overnight in cold water. Drain and place in a large saucepan. Cover with cold water, bring to the boil and skim well. Add halved onions and halved carrots, peppercorns and herbs. Cover with a tight-fitting lid and simmer for 2½ hours. Remove meat from saucepan. Serve hot with vegetables or cold with green salad.

Orange Brisket

2 lb/1 kg rolled brisket beef
2 tablespoons oil
1 cup/½ pint/250 ml cider
2 garlic cloves
2 onions
Sprig of parsley
Sprig of thyme
1 bay leaf
½ cup/¼ pint/125 ml stock
1 orange
Salt and pepper
2 teaspoons cornstarch
1 tablespoon cold water

Mix oil and cider and put into deep casserole with crushed garlic, sliced onion, herbs and a few orange slices. Add brisket and marinate for 3–4 hours, turning frequently. Add stock and seasoning, cover and cook slowly at 325°F/170°C/Gas Mark 3 for 2½ hours until tender. Remove brisket and keep warm. Strain liquid into clean pan, thicken with cornstarch blended with water, bring to boil and simmer for about 5 minutes. Serve brisket with sauce garnished with remaining orange slices.

Beef with Sweet and Sour Cabbage

2 lb/1 kg topside beef (round)
2 tablespoons dripping(s)
1 large onion
1 small white cabbage
⅓ cup/2 oz/50 g seedless raisins
⅓ cup/2 oz/50 g soft brown sugar
½ cup/¼ pint/125 ml red wine vinegar
½ cup/¼ pint/125 ml beef stock
Salt and pepper

Melt dripping(s) in a frying pan, and brown beef on all sides. Remove meat and fry sliced onion and finely sliced cabbage until pale brown. Add the raisins and brown sugar and stir well. Put cabbage mixture into a large casserole. Hollow out the center, and put the beef in the middle. Pour vinegar and stock over the roast and season well. Cover with a tight-fitting lid and bake at 325°F/170°C/Gas Mark 3 for 2½ hours. When cooked remove the meat and cut into slices. Serve with the cabbage.

Braised Brisket with Stuffed Onions

3 lb/1.5 kg rolled brisket
2 tablespoons dripping(s)
4 large onions
3 slices of bacon (streaky)
1 tablespoon breadcrumbs
Salt and pepper
2 tablespoons melted butter

Remove the centers from the onions. Chop the bacon and mix with the breadcrumbs, salt, pepper and butter. Fill the onions with the stuffing. Place remaining stuffing in spaces in brisket. Make sure roast is well tied and brown all sides in hot dripping(s) in a heavy pan. Remove and wrap in two layers of cooking foil, sealing the edges firmly. Place in a dry roasting pan. Bake at 450°F/230°C/Gas Mark 8 for 2 hours. Bake onions for final 40 minutes on a lower shelf. Serve meat with onions and juices from foil.

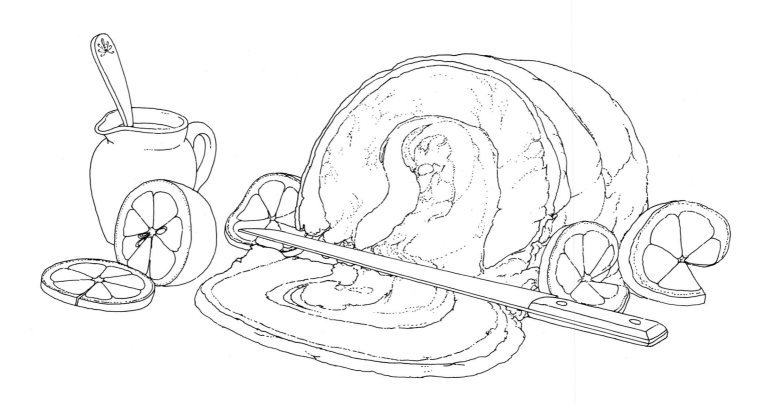

Ground Cobbler

Illustrated on page 32

1 lb/450 g ground beef
1 large onion
2 tablespoons butter or margarine
1¼ cups/4 oz/100 g mushrooms
5 tablespoons plain (all-purpose) flour
1 beef stock cube
14 oz/400 g can of tomatoes
1 tablespoon concentrated tomato paste
1 teaspoon mixed dried herbs
Pinch of sugar
2 teaspoons dry mustard

Topping
2 cups/8 oz/225 g
self-raising (self-rising) flour
½ teaspoon salt
¼ cup/2 oz/50 g margarine
½ cup/¼ pint/125 ml milk
¾ cup/3 oz/75 g grated cheese
Egg or milk for glazing

Chop the onion and soften in the butter or margarine. Add the beef and cook for 5 minutes, turning often. Add the chopped mushrooms and cook for 3 minutes. Sprinkle in the flour, stir well and take off the heat. Add the crumbled stock cube, tomatoes and their juice, tomato paste, herbs, sugar and mustard. Bring to the boil, stirring all the time. Season with salt and pepper, reduce heat and cook gently for 10 minutes. Turn into an ovenproof dish. Prepare the topping by sifting flour and salt and rubbing in the margarine until the mixture looks like breadcrumbs. Stir in milk and mix well to form a soft dough. Knead lightly on a floured board and then roll out to an oblong 15 × 7 in (37.5 × 17.5 cm). Sprinkle with cheese and roll up loosely lengthways. Cut into 12 slices and put these overlapping around the edge of the dish. Brush with beaten egg or milk. Bake at 400°F/200°C/Gas Mark 6 for 30 minutes until the topping is golden brown.

Beef Goulash

1½ lb/675 g chuck or blade steak
¼ cup/2 oz/50 g dripping(s)
2 onions
1 garlic clove
2 teaspoons paprika
½ teaspoon cayenne pepper
1 tablespoon plain (all-purpose) flour
2 cups/1 pint/500 ml stock
2 tablespoons tomato purée
Salt and pepper
½ cup/¼ pint/125 ml natural yogurt

Brown cubed meat in hot dripping(s) in a casserole, then remove. Fry sliced onion, crushed garlic, paprika, cayenne and flour for 1 minute. Return meat to the casserole and add stock, purée and seasoning. Cover and simmer for 2 hours. Stir in yogurt immediately before serving.

Beef Curry

1½ lb/675 g shin beef (foreshank)
3 tablespoons oil
1 large onion
2 garlic cloves
1 tablespoon curry powder
2 cups/1 pint/500 ml beef stock
1 small apple
⅓ cup/2 oz/50 g sultanas (raisins)

Heat the oil in a frying pan and fry the chopped onion and crushed garlic until soft but not brown. Add the cubed beef and brown on all sides. Stir in the curry powder and fry stirring continuously for 5 minutes. Gradually stir in the stock. Cover and simmer gently for 1½ hours. Add the grated apple and sultanas or raisins and cook for 30 minutes. Serve with boiled rice.

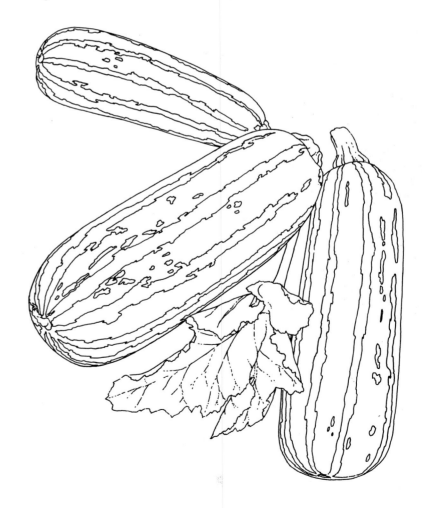

Spiced Topside

2 lb/1 kg topside beef (round)
6 slices of lean bacon
1 small onion
2 cups/1 pint/500 ml brown ale (beer)
2 cups/1 pint/500 ml water
2 teaspoons salt
2 tablespoons vinegar

Arrange bacon and chopped onion in bottom of deep pan. Add meat, ale, water and salt. Cover pan and simmer for 1½ hours until tender. Take out the meat and slice. Heat gravy for a few minutes and pour over meat. Any surplus cooking liquid makes a delicious stock for soup.

Beef and Apple Stew

1½ lb/675 g shin (shank) beef
¼ cup/1 oz/25 g plain (all-purpose) flour
1 teaspoon dry mustard
1 teaspoon mixed herbs
Salt and pepper
¼ cup/2 oz/50 g dripping(s)
2 onions
2 carrots
2 tablespoons vinegar
1¼ cups/4 oz/100 g mushrooms
1½ cups/¾ pint/375 ml stock
1 large cooking apple

Toss cubed meat in seasoned flour and fry in hot dripping(s). Remove meat and fry the sliced onions and carrots until golden brown. Remove onions and carrots, add vinegar to fat and boil until vinegar has almost evaporated. Add stock. Place meat, fried vegetables and sliced mushrooms in casserole, and pour the hot stock over them. Cover tightly and cook at 325°F/170°C/Gas Mark 3 for 2½ hours. Peel and core apple and cut in thin slices. Add apple slices and cook for 30 minutes.

Winter Beef Roll

1 skirt beef (boneless flank) max 3–4 lb
½ lb/225 g minced (ground) pork
1 egg
1 teaspoon chopped parsley
1 beef cube
¼ cup/1 oz/25 g grated cheese
Salt and pepper
1 potato
1 onion

Slit the skirt (flank) down the middle, taking care that only one side is opened. Mix pork, egg, parsley and cheese, and add salt and pepper. Fill skirt (flank) with this mixture, and sew up slit with thread. Put in a saucepan with potato and onion and a crumbled beef cube. Just cover with water. Bring to the boil, then lower the heat and simmer for 1½ hours or until the meat is tender. When ready, take the beef roll out of the soup and cut into slices. Serve soup with fried or toasted bread cubes. Serve sliced beef with vegetables.

Jugged Beef

1½ lb/675 g shin beef (foreshank)
½ cup/2 oz/50 g seasoned flour
6 slices of lean bacon
2 onions stuck with 4 cloves
Grated rind ½ lemon
Sprig of parsley
Sprig of thyme
1 bay leaf
6 small mushrooms
1½ cups/¾ pint/275 ml strong beef stock

Cut meat into 2-in/5-cm pieces and roll in the seasoned flour. Fry chopped bacon in a saucepan, and add the meat, browning lightly. Add onions, lemon rind, herbs, mushrooms and stock. Cover and cook slowly either on the top of the stove or in a casserole at 300°F/150°C/Gas Mark 2 for 3 hours. Remove herbs and onions before serving.

Meat and Vegetable Loaf

2 cups/1 lb/450 g raw minced (ground) beef
3 cups/6 oz/175 g fresh white breadcrumbs
½ lb/225 g carrots
1 small onion
½ green pepper
1 tablespoon Worcestershire sauce
1 tablespoon tomato purée
1 teaspoon prepared mustard
1 teaspoon mixed herbs
1 egg
Salt and pepper

Line base of a greased 6-in/15-cm cake pan with greaseproof (wax) paper. Grate the carrots, and chop the onion and pepper. Thoroughly combine all ingredients and spoon into the pan leveling down well with the back of a spoon. Cover with cooking foil. Bake at 350°F/180°C/Gas Mark 4 for 1¼–1½ hours. Leave to cool in the pan weighted down on top. Turn out on to a serving dish and serve with salad.

Spanish Country Casserole

Illustrated on pages 28/29

1½ lb/675 g shin beef (foreshank)
1 tablespoon oil
1 tablespoon butter
3 carrots
1 onion
1 garlic clove
2 tablespoons plain (all-purpose) flour
½ cup/¼ pint/125 ml dry white wine
1 cup/½ pint/250 ml chicken stock
15 oz/425 g can tomatoes
Sprig of parsley
1 bay leaf
Salt and pepper
8 Spanish stuffed green olives

Cut beef into 1½-in/3.75-cm cubes. Heat the oil, add the butter and fry half the meat at a time, over a moderate heat, turning once, until golden. Drain meat well and put into a casserole. Slice the carrots and chop the onions. Put into the fat with the crushed garlic and fry lightly for 5 minutes. Sprinkle the flour on the vegetables and continue to cook, stirring well, until the flour has browned. Mix in wine, stock, tomatoes with juice, parsley, bay leaf, salt and pepper. Bring to boiling point and pour over the meat. Cover the casserole and cook at 325°F/170°C/Gas Mark 3 for 2½ hours. Stir in sliced olives just before serving.

Beef Roll

¾ lb/350 g raw minced (ground) beef
1 cup/2 oz/50 g fresh white breadcrumbs
2 teaspoons horseradish sauce
1 tablespoon tomato ketchup
1 teaspoon salt
1 egg
3 cups/12 oz/350 g pastry

Roll pastry into a rectangle, approximately 10 × 8 in/25 × 20 cm. Brush lightly with beaten egg. Mix all other ingredients together well and shape into a roll, 9 in/22.5 cm in length. Stand meat roll in the middle of the pastry and wrap the pastry round it. Press join and ends of pastry together well to seal, then transfer to a greased baking tray with join underneath. Using the back of a knife, make criss-cross lines over the top to form a diamond pattern. Brush with beaten egg and bake at 425°F/220°C/Gas Mark 7 for 20 minutes, then at 375°F/190°C/Gas Mark 5 for 25 minutes. Serve, cut in slices, either hot or cold.

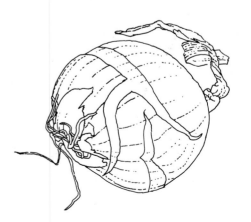

Spring Beef Casserole

Recipe on page 27

Chuck or blade steak
Seasoned flour
Oil
Onions
Carrots
Small celeriac (celery root)
Can of tomatoes
Beef stock
Worcestershire sauce
Salt and pepper
Parsley
Thyme
Bay leaf
Stuffed green olives

Dutch Meatballs

1 lb/450 g raw minced (ground) beef
½ cup/2 oz/50 g white breadcrumbs
1 small onion
1 egg
Salt and pepper
3 tablespoons oil
1 large onion
¼ cup/4 oz/100 g mushrooms
1 tablespoon plain (all-purpose) flour
1 cup/½ pint/250 ml stock
1 tablespoon tomato purée
¾ cup/2 oz/50 g shell-shaped noodles

Mix together meat, half the breadcrumbs, small grated onion, egg and seasoning, and form into 12 balls. Roll balls in the remaining breadcrumbs. Heat the oil and fry the balls turning frequently for 15 minutes. Remove from the frying pan, place in a casserole and keep warm. Fry the sliced large onion in the same pan and when soft add the sliced mushrooms. Fry for a further 2 minutes. Remove from the pan and add to the meatballs in the casserole. Stir the flour into the remaining oil in the pan, loosening any brown particles stuck to the bottom. Cook for 3 minutes. Gradually pour in the stock off the heat. Stir in the tomato purée. Return to the heat and cook thoroughly. Pour the gravy into the casserole. Cover and cook at 350°F/180°C/Gas Mark 4 for 30 minutes. Before serving, stir in the cooked noodles.

Spanish Hash

1 lb/450 g raw minced (ground) beef
1 cup/6 oz/175 g chick peas
1 medium onion
2 tablespoons oil
1 tablespoon tomato purée
1 lb/450 g can of tomatoes
1 cup/½ pint/250 ml beef stock
⅓ cup/2 oz/50 g Spanish stuffed olives
¼ cup/1 oz/25 g raisins

Soak the peas overnight in cold water. Chop the onion and fry in oil for 3 minutes. Add the beef and cook until lightly browned. Stir in tomato purée and canned tomatoes. Add the stock, stir well, and add the drained peas, halved olives and raisins. Cover and simmer for 1 hour.

Aberdeen Sausage

2 lb/1 kg chuck, shoulder or blade beef
12 slices of lean bacon
1 small onion
¾ cup/4 oz/100 g porridge oats
1 tablespoon Worcestershire sauce
1 egg
Salt and pepper
1 teaspoon mixed herbs

Grind the beef, bacon and onion twice. Add the other ingredients and mix well. Shape into a long thick sausage and wrap in foil. Put on a baking sheet and bake at 325°F/170°C/Gas Mark 3 for 2 hours. Serve cold.

Beef and Bacon Slice

1 lb/450 g minced (ground) beef
1¾ cups/12 oz/350 g
very finely chopped bacon pieces
(15 slices approx)
2 slices white bread
Black pepper
1 teaspoon mixed herbs
1 tablespoon rolled oats
1 egg
1 beef cube
1 bay leaf

Mix beef, bacon and bread, and add black pepper, mixed herbs, rolled oats, crumbled stock cube and egg and mix thoroughly. Place mixture on top of a bay leaf in an ovenware dish. Cover with foil and place in a saucepan of water to give water level approximately half-way up container. Steam with a close-fitting lid for 2½ hours. Serve hot or cold.

Celebration Steak

1 lb/450g rump (round) steak or sirloin
2 tablespoons butter
1¼ cups/4 oz/100 g mushrooms
1 garlic clove
A little olive oil
Salt and pepper
1 teaspoon chopped parsley
5 tablespoons cream

Beat the steak to tenderize it. (Sirloin steak does not need to be tenderized.) Melt butter in a frying pan, add sliced mushrooms, crushed garlic and seasoning. Fry until tender. Remove mushrooms and keep them hot. Brush both sides of steak with oil. Fry it on both sides in the butter in the pan. Add parsley, mushrooms and cream, heat gently and serve hot.

Chinese Beef and Mushrooms

1 lb/450g sirloin or rump beef
1 green pepper
¼ cup/2 oz/50 g butter
1¼ cups/4 oz/100 g mushrooms
1 garlic clove

Sauce
¼ cup/2 oz/50 g sugar
1 cup/½ pint/250 ml stock
3 tablespoons vinegar
2 tablespoons sherry
½ teaspoon soy sauce
1 tablespoon cornstarch
2 tablespoons cold water

Slice the beef thinly. Cut pepper into small squares and cook in boiling water for 10 minutes. Dissolve the sugar in the stock. Add the vinegar, sherry, soy sauce and the cornstarch blended with the water to the stock. Bring all ingredients to the boil. Boil gently for 2–3 minutes stirring continuously. Place to one side. Fry the beef in the butter for 5 minutes turning frequently. Add the sliced mushrooms and crushed garlic and fry for a further 5 minutes. Add the drained pepper. Pour the sauce over the meat, mushrooms and pepper and heat through thoroughly. Serve with boiled or fried rice.

Beef Chasseur

1½ lb/675 g raw minced (ground) beef
1 large onion
1 teaspoon Worcestershire sauce
4 thick slices white bread
Cooking oil
2 tablespoons butter
1 tablespoon plain (all-purpose) flour
½ cup/¼ pint/125 ml red wine
3 tomatoes
2 teaspoons tomato purée
1 garlic clove
Pinch of mixed herbs
1 cup/½ pint/250 ml stock
1¾ cups/6 oz/175 g mushrooms

Put aside 2 tablespoons of chopped onion. Mix the meat with the rest of the onion and the Worcestershire sauce. Season with salt and pepper. Divide into four portions and shape each into a large round. Cut the bread into rounds, slightly larger than the beef. Preheat the oven to its lowest setting. Heat a little cooking oil in a pan and fry the bread rounds until crisp and golden brown on both sides. Keep warm in the oven. Pour away oil but leave 2 tablespoons in the pan. Add the butter to the pan. Fry the beef rounds until well browned on both sides. Keep warm while making the sauce. Fry remaining onion in the fat left in the pan until soft. Stir in the flour and cook for several minutes, stirring well. Remove the pan from the heat and gradually add the wine, skinned and seeded tomatoes, purée, crushed garlic, stock and herbs.

Stir over medium heat until the sauce comes to the boil and thickens. Season with salt and pepper. Fry the mushrooms in a knob of butter for a minute. To serve, place the fried bread rounds on a hot serving dish and top each with a beef round. Garnish with the fried mushrooms and serve with the sauce.

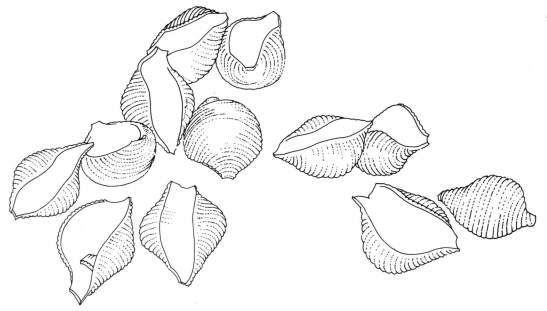

Smothered Beef

Recipe on page 23

Stewing beef
Oil
Onions
Can of condensed tomato soup
Celery salt
Mustard
Rosemary
Salt and pepper
Stuffed green olives

Spicy Beef Ball Skewers

Skewers

1 lb/450g raw minced (ground) beef
1 cup/2oz/50g fresh white breadcrumbs
1 tablespoon chopped parsley
1 tablespoon Worcestershire sauce
Salt and pepper
3 medium onions

Baste

2 tablespoons Worcestershire sauce
6 tablespoons tomato ketchup
½ teaspoon prepared mustard
1 tablespoon soft brown sugar
2 teaspoons lemon juice
2 tablespoons water

Combine beef, breadcrumbs, parsley, sauce and seasonings. Form into 16 balls approximately the size of a walnut. Parboil onions for 5 minutes. Cut each onion into four wedges. Thread meatballs on to four skewers alternating with onion wedges and starting and finishing with a meatball. Combine all the basting ingredients in a saucepan and heat, stirring, to dissolve sugar. Cook gently for 3 minutes. Brush prepared skewers with baste mixture. Place skewers under hot grill (broiler) for about 10 minutes turning them once. Serve with green salad.

Beef Olives

1 lb/450g topside beef (round or rump)
8 slices unsmoked bacon (streaky)
1 medium onion
2 small gherkins
1 teaspoon mixed herbs
¼ cup/2oz/50g butter
1 cup/½ pint/250ml stock
A little cornstarch

Cut the beef into 8 thin slices. Stretch the bacon with the back of a knife and put a slice on each slice of the beef. Sprinkle with finely chopped onion, gherkin and herbs. Roll up and tie with string or secure with toothpick. Brown gently all over in butter for about 10 minutes. Add the hot stock, cover and continue cooking for 10 minutes until the meat is tender. Thicken the liquid with a little cornstarch and cook for 5 minutes. Remove string or toothpicks before serving.

Kebabs with Olives

Illustrated on page 81

1 lb/450g rump (round) steak
4 slices of bacon (streaky)
8 small tomatoes
8 button mushrooms
8 Spanish stuffed green olives
A little oil
1¼ cups/6oz/175g long-grain rice

Barbecue Sauce

1 tablespoon oil
1 medium onion
1 tablespoon plain (all-purpose) flour
½ cup/¼ pint/125ml water
1 tablespoon tomato purée
1 tablespoon red currant jelly
1 tablespoon vinegar
1 tablespoon Worcestershire sauce
1 tablespoon finely chopped green pepper

Stretch bacon with the back of a knife, cut each in half and roll up. Trim steak and cut into 1-in/2.5-cm cubes. Thread steak and bacon on to 4 skewers. Thread tomatoes, mushrooms and olives on to 4 skewers, alternating them. Brush all with oil and grill (broil), turning, until cooked. The vegetables will cook more quickly and should be removed and kept hot when done. Serve on a bed of cooked rice, accompanied by the sauce.

To make the Barbecue Sauce: heat the oil and fry the chopped onion until lightly browned. Stir in flour and cook for 1 minute. Add water, stirring until thickened. Add purée, jelly, vinegar and Worcestershire sauce. Cook together for 10 minutes. Stir in peppers and serve.

Meatballs with Olives

Illustrated on pages 52/53

¾ lb/350g finely ground lean beef
1 egg
¼ teaspoon dried mixed herbs
1 teaspoon salt
Black pepper
18 Spanish stuffed green olives
Plain (all-purpose) flour
2 tablespoons oil
2 onions
10½ oz/298 g can of condensed oxtail soup
1 teaspoon Worcestershire sauce

Beat the egg lightly in a bowl. Add the beef, herbs and seasonings and mix well together. Drain the olives and dry on paper towel. Firmly wrap a little beef mixture around each olive. Coat the meatballs in a little flour. Heat the oil and fry the meatballs until brown. Remove and put on one side. Add the sliced onions to the oil remaining in the pan and fry for 3–4 minutes. Drain off any excess oil, add the soup with the Worcestershire sauce and bring to the boil. Return the meatballs to the pan, cover and simmer for 30 minutes.

Kidney Beef Pudding

½ lb/225 g minced (ground) raw beef
6 slices of lean bacon
1 pig's kidney
1 tablespoon seasoned flour
2 tomatoes
1 small onion
½ cup/¼ pint/125 ml stock
Salt and pepper
3 cups/12 oz/350 g
self-raising (self-rising) flour
1½ cups/6 oz/175 g shredded suet

Make suet pastry by mixing flour and suet and mixing to a soft dough with cold water. Roll out two-thirds of the pastry and use to line a well-buttered 4 cup/2 pint/1 liter pudding basin (steaming mold). Toss all the chopped meat in seasoned flour. Fill the lined basin (mold) with meat, chopped tomatoes, chopped onion and stock. Season to taste. Cover with lid rolled from remaining pastry, sealing pastry edges well together. Cover top with a piece of buttered cooking foil and steam for 2 hours. Serve from the bowl without turning out.

Queensland Casserole

2 lb/1 kg chuck or blade steak
2 onions
2 tablespoons butter
1 tablespoon olive oil
1 tablespoon seasoned flour
8 oz/225 g can of pineapple pieces
1 cup/½ pint/250 ml red wine
1 cup/½ pint/250 ml beef stock
Salt and pepper
2 tablespoons chopped parsley

Fry chopped onions in butter and oil until transparent. Push to one side of pan. Dip cubed meat pieces in seasoned flour and fry until golden brown all over. Add drained pineapple pieces, wine and stock. Cover and simmer gently until meat is tender, for about 1¼ hours. Serve on plain boiled rice, topped with chopped parsley.

Beef Stroganoff

12 oz/350g rump or sirloin steak
3 shallots
⅓ cup/3 oz/75 g butter
½ cup/¼ pint/125 ml cream

Cut steak into fine slices and cook for 5 minutes in butter. Add salt and pepper and add finely chopped shallots. When shallots are soft add the cream, mix well and serve with rice.

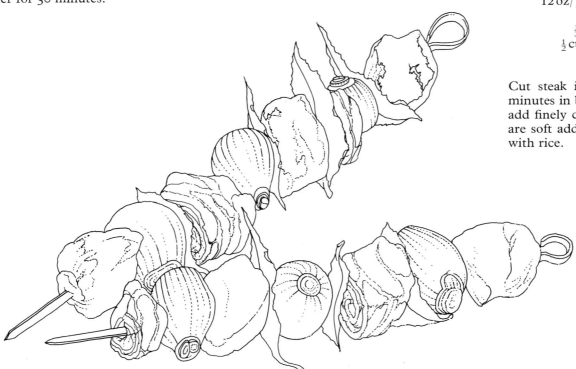

Beef Casserole with Noodles

Recipe on page 22

Chuck or blade steak
Dripping(s)
Leeks
Tomatoes
Salt and pepper
Cider
Cheddar cheese
Noodles

Beef and Mushroom Pudding

1 lb/450 g chuck or blade steak
2 cups/8 oz/225 g
self-raising (self-rising) flour
1 cup/4 oz/100 g shredded suet
6 tablespoons water
¼ lb/4 oz/100 g kidneys
¼ cup/1 oz/25 g plain (all-purpose) flour
1 tablespoon dry mustard
1¼ cups/4 oz/100 g mushrooms
½ cup/¼ pint/125 ml beef stock

Sift the flour into a bowl, add the suet, season well with salt and pepper, stir in the water and mix to a firm paste. Knead lightly on a floured surface, shape into a ball, cover with the mixing bowl and leave for 10 minutes before using. Line a 3 cup/1½ pint/750 ml greased pudding basin (steaming mold) with two-thirds of the pastry. Cube the steak and core and chop the kidneys. Mix the plain (all-purpose) flour with the mustard powder and toss the steak and kidney in this seasoned flour. Add the mushrooms and mix well. Put the meat mixture in the basin (mold) and season with salt and pepper. Add the stock. Use the remaining pastry to make a lid and seal the edges well. Cover with foil and steam for 4 hours.

Beef Flamenco

1 lb/450 g shin (foreshank) of beef
1 tablespoon cooking oil
2 slices of bacon (streaky)
2 cups/12 oz/350 g onions
¼ cup/1 oz/25 g plain (all-purpose) flour
15 oz/425 g can of tomatoes
2 cups/1 pint/500 ml beef stock
2 tablespoons Worcestershire sauce
Salt and pepper
¾ lb/350 g potatoes
8 stuffed olives

Heat oil in pan and fry chopped bacon and chopped onions for 3 minutes. Add cubed beef and cook to brown on all sides. Stir in flour and then add tomatoes with juice, Worcestershire sauce and stock. Bring to boil, stirring, and add seasoning. Cover and simmer gently for 2 hours. Alternatively transfer to a casserole and cook at 325°F/170°C/Gas Mark 3 for 2 hours. Add cubed potatoes and whole olives and cook for 30 minutes.

Meatball Batter Pudding

¾ lb/350 g raw minced (ground) beef
1 cup/2 oz/50 g fresh white breadcrumbs
1 medium onion
¼ teaspoon mixed herbs
1 tablespoon tomato purée
2 teaspoons Worcestershire sauce

Batter
1 cup/4 oz/100 g plain (all-purpose) flour
½ teaspoon salt
1 egg
1 cup/½ pint/250 ml milk

Grate onion and combine ingredients for meatballs. Form into a large sausage and divide into 8 portions. Shape into balls and place in greased, shallow ovenproof dish. Preheat oven to 425°F/220°C/Gas Mark 7. Combine flour and salt in a bowl. Add egg yolk and half the liquid and beat until smooth. Stir in remaining milk. Beat egg white until nearly stiff and fold into batter. Pour over meatballs and bake at 425°F/220°C/Gas Mark 7 for 45 minutes, until well risen and golden brown.

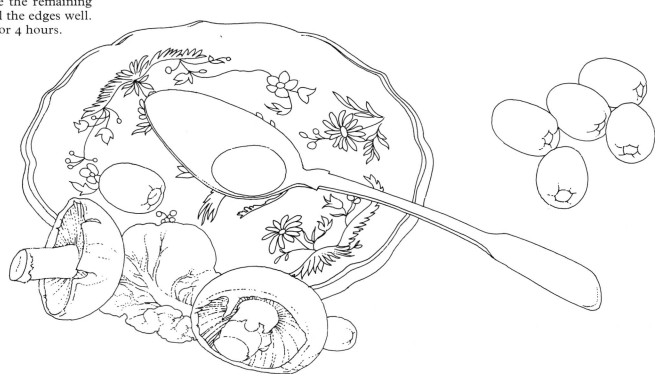

Upside-down Beef

¾ lb/350 g raw minced (ground) beef
2 lb/1 kg potatoes
2 tablespoons cooking fat
1 medium onion
2 tablespoons chutney
1 tablespoon chopped parsley
Salt and pepper
3 carrots
1 tablespoon milk
1 tablespoon margarine

Melt the fat in a saucepan. Add the chopped onion and fry, without browning, until tender. Add the beef, chutney, parsley and seasoning. Slice the carrots thinly and arrange in rows in the base of the casserole. Cream the potatoes with the milk, margarine and seasoning. Spread half over the carrots; put the meat on top and cover with the remaining potato. Bake at 375°F/190°C/ Gas Mark 5 for 30 minutes. When cooked, allow to cool for 5 minutes before turning out on to a warm serving dish.

Beef and Tomato Pie

½ lb/225 g cooked beef
2 tablespoons butter
2 large onions
3 hard-boiled eggs
4 tomatoes
Prepared mustard
Salt and pepper

Cheese sauce
¼ cup/1 oz/25 g plain (all-purpose) flour
2 tablespoons butter
1 cup/½ pint/250 ml milk
¾ cup/3 oz/75 g cheese

Melt butter in a frying pan and add sliced onions. Cook till golden brown. Grease an ovenproof dish and line with onion, then place a layer of sliced egg and sliced tomato on top of the onion. Season, and add a layer of thinly sliced meat. Spread with a little mustard. Repeat until all ingredients are used, saving a little of the tomato for garnish. Make cheese sauce by melting butter and working in flour. Stir in milk and heat gently until smooth. Remove from heat and stir in grated cheese. Pour sauce over the top. Bake at 400°F/200°C/Gas Mark 6 for 30 minutes. Before serving, decorate pie with tomato.

Savory Beef Envelopes

Illustrated on pages 56/57

1 cup/½ lb/225 g
fresh minced (ground) beef
1 tablespoon lard
1 small onion
⅔ cup/2 oz/50 g mushrooms
2 tablespoons plain (all-purpose) flour
½ cup/¼ pint/125 ml stock
1 teaspoon prepared mustard
1 tablespoon tomato purée
Pinch of mixed herbs
Salt and pepper
½ lb/225 g sausagemeat
3 cups/¾ lb/350 g pastry
1 egg

Melt lard in a saucepan, and gently fry finely chopped onion and mushrooms until tender. Add ground beef and brown lightly all over. Stir in flour and cook for 1 minute. Remove from heat and gradually stir in stock, mustard, tomato purée, herbs and seasoning. Return to heat and bring to the boil, stirring. Cook gently for 5 minutes, stirring occasionally. Remove from heat and stir in sausagemeat, mixing well. Leave mixture until cold. Roll out pastry on a floured board to a large square, and cut into four 6-in/15-cm squares. Divide meat mixture into four, and pile in the center of each square of pastry. Moisten edges of pastry with water, and draw edges up into the center to form an envelope shape. Press edges well together, and crimp a decorative edge. Brush with beaten egg and bake at 400°F/200°C/Gas Mark 6 for 30 minutes. Reduce heat to 350°F/180°C/Gas Mark 4 and continue cooking for a further 20 minutes until golden brown and filling is tender.

Steak and Onion Pie

Recipe on page 49

Chuck or blade steak
Seasoned flour
Dripping(s)
Onions
Mushrooms
Stock
Puff pastry
Egg

Olde English Steak and Kidney Pie

Illustrated on pages 56/57

1½ lb/675 g stewing steak
¼ cup/1 oz/25 g plain (all-purpose) flour
Salt and pepper
½ lb/225 g kidney
2 tablespoons lard
1 medium onion
1¼ cups/4 oz/100 g button mushrooms
1 cup/½ pint/250 ml stock
3 cups/12 oz/350 g puff pastry
1 egg

Put flour and plenty of seasoning in a plastic bag. Add cubed steak and kidney and shake bag until all meat is coated with flour. Reserve any flour in the bag and remove meat. Melt lard and fry chopped onion until just tender, but not brown. Add meat and brown quickly on all sides. Add sliced mushrooms, and cook for 1 minute. Stir in reserved flour, if any, then add stock, stirring. Bring to the boil, cover and simmer gently for 1½–2 hours or until meat is tender. Put meat and mushrooms into a deep pie dish or casserole (approximately 6 inches deep), with enough gravy to come halfway up the dish.

Roll out pastry to about 1 in/2.5 cm larger than top of pie dish. Cut out a long strip of pastry about ½ in/1.25 cm wide to fit rim of dish and a pastry lid. Moisten rim of dish and press on pastry strip. Moisten pastry strip and place lid on dish. Press down well, to seal edges, trim off excess pastry, then knock edges together and flute with a knife. Re-roll trimmings and cut out pastry leaves to decorate pie. Brush with beaten egg, place dish on a baking sheet and bake at 425°F/220°C/Gas Mark 7 for 20 minutes. Reduce heat to 350°F/180°C/Gas Mark 4 and cook for a further 15 minutes.

Steak and Onion Pie

Illustrated on page 48

1½ lb/675 g chuck or blade steak
1 tablespoon seasoned flour
2 tablespoons dripping(s)
2 onions
1¼ cups/4 oz/100 g mushrooms
1 cup/½ pint/500 ml stock
3 cups/12 oz/350 g puff pastry
1 egg

Coat cubed meat in seasoned flour and fry in hot dripping(s) until brown. Remove from frying pan and put into saucepan. Fry sliced onion until soft; add sliced mushrooms and fry for a further 2 minutes. Add to meat. Pour in stock, cover and simmer for 1½ hours. Leave to cool then place in a pie dish with liquid to come halfway up the dish. Cover with pastry, seal edges and glaze with egg. Bake at 425°F/220°C/Gas Mark 7 for 30 minutes.

Fillet of Beef in Pastry

1½ lb/675 g fillet (tenderloin) of beef
A little oil
1 garlic clove
Salt and pepper
⅓ cup/3 oz/75 g smooth liver pâté
⅓ cup/2 oz/50 g stuffed green olives
2 cups/8 oz/225 g puff pastry
1 egg

Trim fillet and tie with string in a neat roll. Brush with oil and insert slivers of garlic. Season, and roast at 425°F/220°C/Gas Mark 7 for 10 minutes. Cool and save meat juices from pan. Remove string. Mix together pâté and sliced olives and spread over top half of fillet. Roll out pastry to oblong four times the width and three times the length of fillet. Trim edges. Place fillet in center, fold pastry over, damping edges to seal and make a complete parcel. Turn over and place with overlapping ends down, on a baking sheet. Roll out trimmings of pastry and cut 4 large leaves. Place on top of fillet to decorate. Brush all over top and sides with egg. Bake at 400°F/200°C/Gas Mark 6 for 40 minutes. Serve with gravy made from meat juices in pan.

Spiced Tattie Pot

1 lb/450 g raw minced (ground) beef
1 tablespoon oil
6 slices of bacon (streaky)
2 large onions
8 oz/225 g can tomatoes
2 tablespoons Worcestershire sauce
1 tablespoon tomato purée
½ teaspoon basil
½ cup/¼ pint/125 ml stock or water
Salt and pepper
1 lb/450 g potatoes
1 tablespoon butter

Heat oil in a large pan, add bacon and 1 chopped onion and fry gently for 5 minutes. Add beef and fry until evenly browned. Add tomatoes, Worcestershire sauce, tomato purée, herbs, stock and seasoning. Bring to the boil, reduce heat and simmer gently for 20 minutes. Slice the second onion and potato and cook in boiling salted water for 3-4 minutes, until potato is just cooked. Drain well.

Spoon half the meat mixture into oven-proof dish and cover with half the potatoes and onion. Spoon remaining meat mixture over the top and overlap rest of potatoes and onion to cover completely. Brush with melted butter and bake at 350°F/180°C/Gas Mark 4 for 1 hour.

Beef and Kidney Roll

¾ lb/350 g raw minced (ground) beef
½ lb/225 g lamb kidneys
2 tablespoons lard
1 large onion
1 tablespoon tomato purée
3 tablespoons chopped parsley
1 teaspoon mixed herbs
10½ oz/298 g can condensed oxtail soup

Pastry
2 cups/8 oz/225 g
self-raising (self-rising) flour
½ teaspoon salt
1 cup/4 oz/100 g shredded suet
7-8 tablespoons water
Milk to glaze

Heat lard in a pan, add chopped onion and fry until softened. Add ground beef and chopped kidneys and fry for 10 minutes until meat is evenly browned. Add tomato purée, herbs and half the soup, and simmer gently for a further 15-20 minutes. Remove from heat and allow to cool.

To make pastry, combine flour, salt and suet in a bowl. Add water and mix to a soft dough. Turn out on to a lightly floured surface and knead lightly. Roll out to ¼ in/0.75 cm thickness and trim to 12 in/30 cm long. Twist strip and place along roll to decorate. Brush pastry with milk. Bake at 400°F/200°C/Gas Mark 6 for 40-45 minutes, until pastry is crisp and golden brown. Heat remaining soup with ½ cup/¼ pint/125 ml water to make sauce and serve separately.

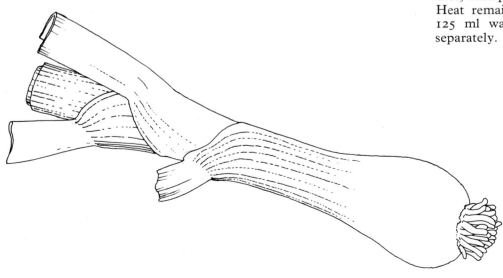

Stir-Fried Beef

Illustrated on pages 24/25

¾ lb/350 g lean beef
3 celery sticks
2 large carrots
6 spring onions (scallions)
4 tablespoons oil
Salt and pepper
Spaghetti or other pasta in tomato sauce

Cut the beef into thin strips. Cut the vegetables into matchstick strips. Fry the vegetables quickly in fat until lightly golden but still crisp. Remove vegetables to a plate and add meat strips to fat in pan. Fry quickly until sealed, brown and just tender. Return vegetables to pan. Season and stir in cooked pasta in tomato sauce. Heat through and serve very hot. Freshly cooked pasta may be used (allow ¾ cup/4 oz/100 g) which has been stirred with 3 tablespoons tomato ketchup. For speed, use a 15 oz/425 g can of pasta in tomato sauce.

Devilled Layer Pudding

Pudding
1½ cups/6 oz/175 g
self-raising (self-rising) flour
1 teaspoon dry mustard
½ teaspoon salt
Pepper
⅓ cup/3 oz/75 g margarine
2 eggs
4 tablespoons milk

Meat
½ lb/225 g cooked minced (ground) meat
5 tablespoons thick gravy
2 teaspoons curry powder
1 small onion
2 eggs
Salt and pepper

Sift flour, mustard, salt and pepper into a bowl. Rub in fat then mix to a soft consistency with the eggs and milk, stirring thoroughly. Blend meat and other ingredients well together and season to taste. Three-quarter fill a well-greased 4 cup/2 pint/1 liter pudding basin (steaming mold) with alternate layers of both mixtures, starting with a layer of meat and finishing with a layer of pudding mixture. Cover basin (mold) with greased foil and steam steadily for 1 hour. Turn out and serve with a well-seasoned hot tomato-flavored sauce.

Meatballs with Olives

Recipe on page 43

Finely ground lean beef
Egg
Dried mixed herbs
Salt and pepper
Stuffed green olives
Flour
Oil
Onions
Can of condensed oxtail soup
Worcestershire sauce

Basic Burger

1 lb/450 g lean minced (ground) beef
1 small onion (optional)
Salt
Pepper
Butter or oil
Egg for binding (optional)

Mix onion (if desired), beef, salt, pepper and egg (if required). Shape into patties (4–6). To cook, grill (broil) for 4–6 minutes turning once, fry in a little oil in a frying pan turning once, or barbecue turning frequently.

101 Burgers

1. Grill (broil) burgers. Top with a slice of cheese. Melt under grill (broiler) and garnish with a slice of tomato.
2. Grill (broil) or fry burgers. Serve with scrambled eggs.
3. Serve with fried onion rings or onion sauce.
4. Serve on a bed of pasta shells mixed with tomato and grated cheese.
5. Cook and halve burgers. Arrange in a split baked potato, garnish with tomato and horseradish sauce.
6. Cook burgers, keep hot. Lightly fry onion and tomato and mix in some cooked sliced green beans.
7. Serve with hot or cold sauerkraut.
8. Serve with salad of orange, tomato, lettuce tossed in French dressing.
9. Serve with curry sauce and plain boiled rice.
10. Cook apple rings with burgers and serve with savory rice.
11. Serve hot burgers with coleslaw salad.
12. Cook rice in stock with peas and slices of red pepper and serve with fried or grilled (broiled) burgers.
13. Try serving burgers with bananas halved and fried.
14. Grill (broil) burgers with bacon wrapped round.
15. Arrange burgers round a mountain of creamy mashed potato and serve peas on top.
16. Add cooked, quartered burgers to an omelette; for extra flavor add fried onions.

17. Spread cream cheese on a hot burger and top with slice of pineapple; flash under a hot grill (broiler).
18. Dip in batter and fry.
19. Make potato cakes and serve with fried burgers.
20. Add mixed herbs to omelette mixture and also add slices of cooked burger.
21. Try macaroni and cheese with cooked burgers.
22. Melt a little red currant jelly, add $\frac{1}{2}$ teaspoon vinegar and reduce. Pour over burgers.
23. Try a burger pan-fry of mushrooms, tomatoes, bacon, sausage and kidney if liked. Serve with fried potatoes.
24. Serve hot burgers on baked beans and sprinkle with hot crushed potato crisps/chips.
25. Arrange hot burgers on cooked spaghetti, cover with tomato sauce and grated cheese.
26. Make pancakes and wrap a cooked burger in each and serve with condensed mushroom soup.
27. Sandwich two burgers together with cream cheese mixed with chopped gherkins.
28. Warm a soft roll or bap and serve a burger inside with fried onion.
29. Take half a soft roll with burger and put a fried egg on top.
30. Fill soft roll with burger and fried bacon.
31. Spread horseradish sauce in a roll and place burger and slices of tomato inside.
32. Top cooked burger with fried eggs and a pineapple ring and serve on a halved roll.
33. Fry burgers, keep hot and cook sliced left-over potato in the pan dripping(s) with leftover cabbage or Brussels sprouts.

34. Make a savory rice with onion, bacon and chopped tomatoes, herbs, and serve with burgers.
35. Cook broad or lima beans, mix with white sauce, serve with burgers and potato croquettes.
36. Cut rounds of puff pastry larger than a burger, and enclose burger and slices of tomato within two rounds. Bake in a hot oven.
37. Try the same thing with horseradish sauce on the burgers.
38. Enclose a large mushroom with a burger in pastry and bake.
39. Try fried onion and bacon with a burger in pastry.
40. Place an uncooked burger on a large round of ordinary pastry, add diced parboiled potato and grated onion, enclose with the edges uppermost in the shape of a Cornish pasty and bake in hot oven.
41. Fry burgers for 5 minutes, allow to cool. Line a round 7-in/17.5-cm pan with ordinary pastry. Put burgers in the bottom, cover with fried onion and tomato and add eggs mixed with milk and seasonings. Bake in hot oven.
42. Lightly fry onion, add chopped tomatoes and a can of drained butter beans, heat and serve with hot burgers.
43. Serve hot burgers with winter salad of diced beets, apple and chopped walnuts.
44. Shredded cabbage, orange segments, tomato tossed in French dressing with hot burgers.
45. Cold diced potato, cold cooked sliced green beans, tomato, tossed in French dressing with hot burgers.

46. Place burgers on baking sheet, fork creamy mashed potato round the edge and break an egg into the center. Bake in moderate oven.
47. Grill (broil) burgers, place a ring of pineapple on top and cover with a cheese slice, grill (broil) to melt the cheese.
48. Slice of bread spread with cream cheese, tomato and hot burger.
49. Slice of bread topped with lettuce, pickled cabbage, hot burger.
50. Spread chutney or pickle on bread, and top with hot burger and raw onion rings.
51. Slice of bread topped with lettuce, potato salad, hot burgers and tomato.
52. Slice of bread topped with lettuce, cream cheese, pineapple and hot burger.
53. Slice of bread topped with potato salad, pickled beet and hot burger.
54. Sandwich a burger between two rounds of bread, buttered sides out. Bake in the oven until crisp.
55. Cook spinach, drain thoroughly, serve with burgers on top with cheese sauce poured over.
56. Alternatively cook spinach, drain, serve with burgers and place a fried egg on each burger.
57. Make Mexican burgers by adding a little curry powder to baked beans and dash of Tabasco sauce with quarters of hot burgers.
58. Blend cream cheese with chopped parsley or chives and mix with creamy mashed potatoes. Sandwich between burgers.
59. Fry small onions and bacon in butter. Cook peas and macaroni and mix with the onions and bacon and serve with burgers.
60. Coat burgers with egg and fresh white breadcrumbs, fry, and serve with hot tomato sauce.

61. Make a favorite stuffing, pile on burgers, garnish with slices of tomato and bake.
62. Fry onions in butter, add finely shredded cabbage, cover and cook until tender. Add sliced red pepper and serve with hot burgers.
63. To make tomato and celery relish, fry onion until soft in butter, add skinned and chopped tomatoes, cook until soft. If liked add some chopped parsley and serve with hot burgers.
64. Brown burgers, remove from pan and add chopped tomatoes, gherkins and diced cucumber. Return burgers to pan and finish cooking until tomatoes are soft.
65. A quick barbecue sauce can be made with a fruit relish, vinegar and Worcestershire sauce to serve with hot grilled (broiled) burgers.
66. Fry burgers in butter and keep hot. To the pan, add a little sugar and some pineapple juice. Dissolve sugar, return burgers to pan and cook for 5 minutes. Heat pineapple and serve with noodles with the sauce poured over the burgers.
67. Brown burgers, remove from pan, add slices of apple and chopped onion. Cook for 5 minutes, add a little cider, return burgers and cook for 10 minutes.
68. Cold burgers with fruit and salad ingredients.
69. Place hot burgers on rounds of toast decorated with slices of orange, cucumber, cocktail onions speared on to a cocktail stick and stuck through the center of a burger.
70. Make a fritter batter and stir in cooked corn. Cook and serve on a dish with burgers and fritters arranged alternately. Serve with fresh tomato sauce.

71. Fry a little onion in butter and add chopped tomatoes and a little stock. Simmer until tomatoes are soft, push through a sieve and reheat. If necessary, thicken with a little blended cornstarch and season to taste. Serve with grilled (broiled) burgers and cooked pasta.
72. Grill (broil) burgers and put a canned apricot on top, just before cooking time is over. The juice could be used for a sauce by adding sugar, and allowing the mixture to reduce. Add a little vinegar to give a slightly piquant flavor and serve with rice.
73. Fry burgers and serve with oxtail soup with a little sherry added to it.
74. Make up a favorite stuffing, form into small balls and fry with burgers, turning all the time. Serve with brown gravy.
75. Serve burgers on a bed of cooked leeks, cover with a cheese sauce and grill (broil).
76. Grill (broil) burgers and place on a serving dish. Heat a small can of favorite soup, pour over burgers and pipe rosettes of hot mashed potato round the dish.
77. Cut burgers into four, arrange alternately on skewers with mushrooms, parboiled onions, bacon, tomatoes and kidneys if liked. Brush with oil and grill (broil) turning frequently. Serve with cooked rice.
78. Fry a little onion in fat and thicken with flour. Add stock and a pinch of curry powder and Worcestershire sauce. Add cooked quartered burgers to the sauce, and serve on slices of toast.
79. Cook thick slices of onion and potato in a little good meat stock. When cooked serve with fried or grilled (broiled) burgers.
80. Serve burgers with baked potatoes and French bread with cheese to follow.

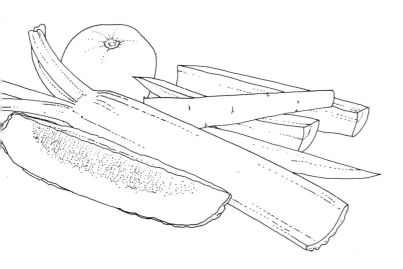

Olde English Steak and Kidney Pie

Recipe on page 49

Stewing steak
Flour
Salt and pepper
Kidney
Lard
Onion
Button mushrooms
Stock
Puff pastry
Egg

Savory Beef Envelopes

Recipe on page 47

Minced/ground beef
Lard
Onion
Mushrooms
Flour
Stock
Mustard
Tomato purée
Mixed herbs
Salt and pepper
Sausagemeat
Pastry
Egg

81. Grill (broil) burgers, top with mashed potato and grated cheese on top and brown under the grill.

82. Fry onion and a little curry powder together. When cooked, add a drained can of butter beans. Heat through and serve with hot burgers.

83. Dip onion rings in a little egg and flour and fry with the burgers, turning frequently.

84. For a really cheap vegetable accompaniment, serve burgers with a mixture of cooked parsnip and turnip, all tossed in a little butter and well seasoned.

85. Try serving burgers with risotto heated through with perhaps some peas added to make a complete dish.

86. Cook whole cabbage leaves. Wrap a cooked burger in each one and serve with tomato sauce.

87. Make a meat and potato hedgehog for the children. Make a short thick cylinder of hot creamy mashed potato and at intervals place in cooked burgers. Serve with cooked halved tomatoes round the dish.

88. Add curry powder to baked beans and serve with hot burgers and fried onion rings.

89. Make a goulash sauce, add yogurt and serve over hot burgers with noodles.

90. Make savory dumplings with cooked onion, bacon and chopped parsley added. When cooked, serve with hot burgers and brown gravy poured over.

91. Grill (broil) burgers, fork mashed potato round edge and grill (broil). Fill center with cooked peas.

92. Layer sliced onion, potatoes and carrots in a casserole ending with a layer of potato. Season well and add a little meat stock, cook in a slow oven for $1\frac{1}{2}$ hours and serve with hot burgers.

93. Dip burgers in egg and coat with a mixture of favorite stuffing and fresh breadcrumbs. Fry and serve with a sauce.

94. Make a thick batter. Place finely chopped onion, tomato and herbs in ovenware dish. Add burgers cut in quarters. Pour over batter and bake in hot oven.

95. Try a fried open sandwich. Fry a slice of bread, and a burger. When nearly cooked, add a pineapple ring and a halved tomato to the pan. Arrange the cooked ingredients on the fried bread.

96. Serve fried burgers with fried bread and fried bananas.

97. Fry burgers and onion rings. Make an omelette with cooked sliced potato, add the onion rings and the burgers cut into quarters.

98. Serve burgers with scrambled egg on top mixed with a few chopped herbs, and serve with French fries.

99. Grill (broil) cheese on toast and serve a hot burger on top; garnish with watercress.

100. Grill (broil) burgers with French mustard spread over and serve with grilled (broiled) tomatoes.

101. Mix sliced eating apples, diced cheese and shredded cabbage with mayonnaise, and serve with hot burger.

Steak Burgers

1 lb/450 g lean minced (ground) beef
1 onion
1 slice of bacon (streaky)
1 tablespoon
Worcestershire or tomato sauce
$\frac{1}{2}$ cup/2 oz/50 g breadcrumbs
1 small egg
Salt and pepper
1 egg
Browned breadcrumbs
Oil or lard for frying

Chop onion and bacon finely. Thoroughly mix first seven ingredients. Flour hands and form mixture into rounds. Coat with egg and breadcrumbs. Grill (broil) for 7 minutes each side under grill (broiler), or fry on both sides in oil or lard.

Swedish Meatballs   Tossed Beef Salad

$\frac{3}{4}$ lb/ 350 g raw minced (ground) beef
$\frac{1}{4}$ lb/ 100 g raw minced (ground) pork
$\frac{1}{2}$ cup/ 2 oz/ 50 g dry white breadcrumbs
1 cup/ $\frac{1}{2}$ pint/ 250 ml creamy milk
1 small onion
1$\frac{1}{2}$ teaspoons salt
$\frac{1}{4}$ teaspoon pepper

3 cups/ 1 lb/ 450 g cold roast beef
2 eating apples
2 celery sticks
4 tomatoes
4 tablespoons chopped parsley
$\frac{1}{2}$ cup/ $\frac{1}{4}$ pint/ 125 ml natural yogurt
Salt and pepper

Mix together the beef and pork. Soak the breadcrumbs in the milk. Chop the onion and cook in a little butter until soft and golden. Mix with meat, soaked breadcrumbs and seasonings until well blended. Shape into 1-in/ 2.5-cm balls. Fry in butter until evenly browned, shaking the pan to keep the balls round. Cook a few at a time, drain well and keep warm. When all the balls are cooked, add a little water to the pan juices and stir well to form a thin gravy to pour over the meatballs. These are also very good in a hot tomato sauce served with pasta.

Dice the beef, apples, celery and tomatoes. Combine beef, apples, celery, tomatoes and parsley in a salad bowl. Pour yogurt over the mixture and season to taste. Chill before serving.

VEAL *American Cuts*

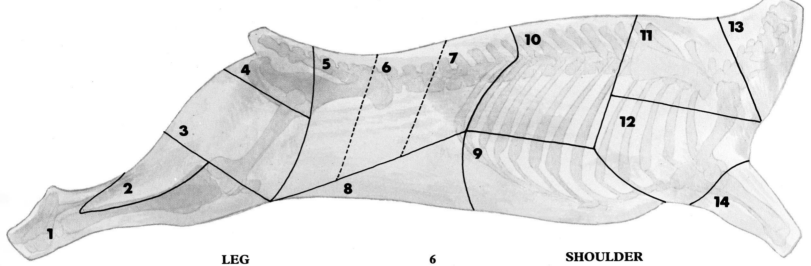

LEG

I
Hind Shank
Hind Shank Pot Roast

2
Heel of Round
Heel of Round Roast

3
Leg
Round Steak (cutlet)
Scallops or cutlet
Leg (Round) Center-Cut Roast
Rosettes or Noisette de Veau

4
Leg
Standing Rump Roast
Rolled Rump Roast

LOIN

5
Sirloin Steak
Sirloin Roast

6
Loin Roast
Loin Chop

7
Kidney Chop
Kidney Roast

FLANK

8
Flank

BREAST

9
Breast Roast
Riblets
Stew Meat
Mock Chicken Legs

RIB

10
Rib Chop
Crown Roast of Veal

SHOULDER

11
Shoulder Blade Roast
Blade Steak
Rolled Shoulder Roast

12
Shoulder
Rolled Shoulder Roast
Arm Roast
Arm Steak

13
Neck
City Chicken
Patties

SHANK

14
Foreshank
Foreshank Roast

British Cuts

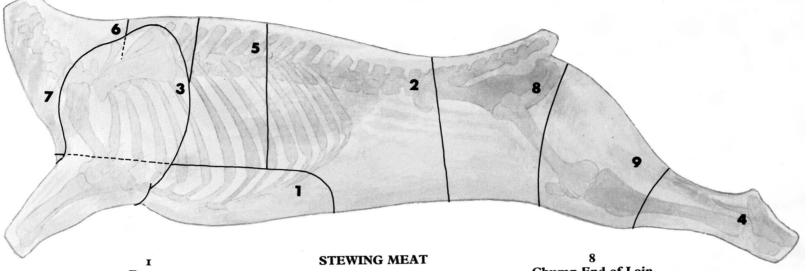

1	STEWING MEAT	8
Breast		**Chump End of Loin**
Rolled Breast Roast	**4**	Fillet of Veal Roast
Breast Roast	**Knuckle**	Fillet of Veal Steak
Stewing/Brasing Meat	Knuckle Roast	Chump Chops
	Stewing Meat	Chump End of Loin Roast
2		
Loin	**5**	
Loin Roast	**Best End Neck**	**ESCALOPES**
Loin Chop	Best End Cutlets	
Boned Loin Roast	Best End Neck Roast	
	Boned and Rolled Best End Neck Roast	**9**
3		**Leg**
Shoulder or Oyster	**6**	Escalopes
Shoulder Roast	**Middle Neck**	Fillet of Veal Roast
Boned and Rolled Shoulder Roast	Middle Neck Roast	Fillet of Veal Steak
	Braising/Stewing meat	Leg Roast
	7	
	Scrag End	
	Stewing or boiling meat	

Veal Sevillana

Illustrated on pages 120/121

4 veal escalopes
½ cup/4 oz/100 g butter
1 medium onion
1¼ cups/4 oz/100 g mushrooms
¾ cup/2 oz/50 g Spanish stuffed green olives
1 cup/2 oz/50 g fresh white breadcrumbs
1 egg
Salt and pepper
6 tablespoons plain (all-purpose) flour
½ cup/¼ pint/125 ml chicken stock
1 orange
1 tablespoon sherry
½ cup/¼ pint/125 ml cream

Melt half the butter in pan, then fry chopped onion until cooked but not colored. Add chopped mushrooms and cook for 2 minutes. Chop half the olives and add to pan with breadcrumbs and egg. Season to taste. Spread mixture on the veal, roll up and secure with string or toothpicks. Melt rest of butter in frying pan and fry rolls until golden and cooked. Put into a serving dish and keep hot. Stir flour into fat remaining in pan and add stock slowly, stirring to blend. Add the juice of the orange, sherry and cream. Pour over the veal rolls. Garnish with remaining olives, halved, and sprinkle thin-cut strips of orange rind on top.

Veal in Tomato Sauce

2 lb/1 kg shoulder of veal
2 tablespoons olive oil
1 garlic clove
2½ cups/8 oz/225 g mushrooms
10 tiny white onions
Salt and pepper
4 large tomatoes
½ cup/¼ pint/125 ml dry white wine
1 cup/½ pint/250 ml chicken stock
Sprig of parsley
Sprig of thyme
1 bay leaf

Cut the veal into cubes and brown in the oil. Lift out veal. Cook the crushed garlic, sliced mushrooms and small whole onions until just soft. Take out the vegetables, mix with the meat in a casserole, and season well. Skin the tomatoes, remove the seeds, and chop the flesh. Stir into the oil and add the wine, stock and herbs. Cook gently until the sauce is smooth. Remove the herbs and pour over the veal and vegetables. Cover and cook at 325°F/170°C/Gas Mark 3 for 1½ hours.

Jellied Veal

½ lb/225 g cooked veal
2 cups/1 pint/500 ml veal stock
1 tablespoon gelatine
1 hard-boiled egg
Salt and pepper

Heat the stock, add seasoning and dissolved gelatine, pour a little of the stock into a mold and chill to set. Chop the veal very finely and put this over the set stock in the mold. Add sliced egg and gradually pour over the remaining stock and replace mold in refrigerator to set. Turn out to serve with salad.

Tarragon Veal

1½ lb/675 g pie veal (stewing veal)
2 tablespoons butter
Flour
1 cup/½ pint/250 ml dry white wine
1 tablespoon chopped tarragon
2 hard-boiled eggs

Cut veal in pieces and brown in butter. Sprinkle with flour and cook till brown. Add wine, and cook at 325°F/170°C/Gas Mark 3 for 1½ hours. Just before serving, stir in chopped tarragon, and garnish with chopped hard-boiled egg.

Spring Veal

1 lb/450 g pie veal (stewing veal)
¼ cup/2 oz/50 g butter
12 small onions
¼ cup/1 oz/25 g plain (all-purpose) flour
2 cups/1 pint/500 ml stock
Salt and pepper
Bunch of mixed herbs
2 lb/1 kg new potatoes
½ lb/225 g French beans (string beans)
1 lb/450 g shelled peas
1 firm lettuce heart
1 lb/450 g new carrots

Cut the meat in small pieces and fry till golden with the whole onions in the butter. Stir in flour, mix well, and add salt and pepper, stock and herbs. Cover and cook at 325°F/170°C/Gas Mark 3 for 1 hour. Cut the beans in chunks, scrape the potatoes and carrots, and cut the lettuce heart in quarters. Add to the casserole, cover and simmer for 1 hour.

Veal Pie

1½ lb/675 g cooked veal
Salt and pepper
1 teaspoon mixed herbs
2 tablespoons water
4 teaspoons gelatine
1 egg
Stock
4 cups/1 lb/450 g pastry

Line inside and bottom of shallow greased pie pan with pastry. Mix chopped meat, herbs and seasoning thoroughly. Fill the pie pan with this mixture and add water. Cover with a pastry lid. Damp and secure the edges well. Make a cut in the center of the pie, brush the pastry with egg and bake at 375°F/190°C/Gas Mark 5 for 1 hour. Dissolve the gelatine in a little stock and pour into the pie through the cut made in the pastry lid. When set, turn out and serve cold.

Fruited Veal in Cream Sauce

4 veal chops
Plain (all-purpose) flour
Salt and pepper
¼ cup/2 oz/50 g butter
⅓ cup/3 fl oz/75 ml white wine
1½ cups/¾ pint/125 ml sour cream
16 oz/450 g can of pear halves
12 prunes (stones removed)

Cut veal into serving-size pieces and dip in seasoned flour. Melt butter in a large pan and cook veal until it is thoroughly browned on all sides. Stir in wine, sour cream and 1 tablespoon syrup from pears. Slice the pear halves and add to pan, together with prunes. Cook gently for 5 minutes. Adjust seasoning and serve with plain boiled rice.

Veal Marengo

1 lb/450 g veal
1 onion
2 tablespoons butter
2 tablespoons flour
Salt and pepper
1 cup/½ pint/250 ml beef stock
2 tablespoons tomato purée
1 bay leaf
1¼ cups/4 oz/100 g mushrooms

Cut the meat into 1-in/2.5-cm pieces. Melt the butter in a frying pan and cook the meat until browned. Add the chopped onion and cook for a few minutes. Blend in flour and transfer ingredients to a saucepan. Add seasoning, tomato purée, bay leaf and stock. Simmer for 1 hour. Add chopped mushrooms and cook for 10 more minutes.

Osso Bucco

2 veal hocks (shin) cut into
3-in/7.5-cm pieces
1 carrot
2 onions
8 oz/225 g can of tomatoes
Sprig of parsley
Sprig of thyme
1 bay leaf
2 tablespoons olive oil
2 beef cubes
Salt and pepper
Grated rind ½ lemon
Parsley

Heat the olive oil and fry the meat, carrot and onions in it until browned. Add the tomatoes, herbs and the beef cubes crumbled and dissolved in 2 cups/1 pint/500 ml hot water. Season with salt and pepper. Cover and cook until tender for 1½ hours. Remove the herbs and serve sprinkled with lemon rind and parsley. Serve with boiled rice and grated Parmesan cheese sprinkled on top.

Swiss Veal

1½ lb/675 g thin veal slices
Seasoned flour
4 tablespoons oil
2 medium onions
1 garlic clove
1 lb/450 g can tomatoes
½ teaspoon sugar
Pinch of rosemary
Pinch of thyme
½ lb/225 g Gruyère cheese
2 tablespoons Parmesan cheese

Coat veal very lightly in seasoned flour and cook until lightly browned in oil. Lift out veal. Slice onions and crush garlic and cook in oil until golden. Purée the tomatoes and add to the onions with the sugar and herbs. Simmer for 5 minutes. Pour half this sauce into a casserole. Top with veal and slices of Gruyère cheese. Pour over remaining sauce and sprinkle with Parmesan cheese. Bake without a lid at 350°F/180°C/Gas Mark 4 for 45 minutes.

LAMB *American Cuts*

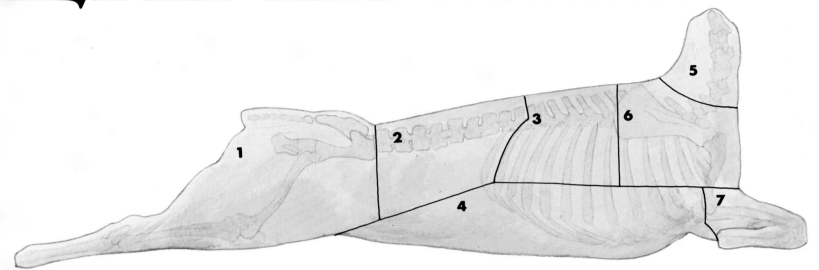

1
Leg
Leg of Lamb Roast
Boneless Sirloin Roast
American Leg Roast
Frenched Leg Roast

2
Loin
Loin Chop
English Chop
Rolled Loin Roast

3
Rib or Rack
Rib Chop
French Rib Chop
Crown Roast of Lamb
Rack of Lamb

4
Breast
Riblets
Rolled Breast Roast
Breast Roast
Stew Meat

5
Neck
Neck Slice

6
Shoulder
Square Cut Shoulder Roast
Blade Chop
Arm Chop
Rolled Shoulder Roast
Boneless Shoulder Roast
Boneless Shoulder Chop
Cushion Shoulder Roast
Saratoga Chops

7
Shank

British Cuts

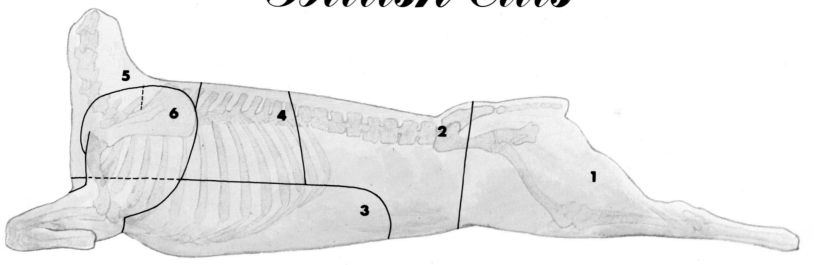

1
Leg
Chump Chops
Leg Roast
Knuckle Roast
Fillet Roast
Lamb Steaks
Stewing Meat
Kebabs

2
Loin
Saddle of Lamb
Loin Chops
Roast of Lamb
Noisettes

3
Breast
Rolled Breast of Lamb Roast

4
Best End of Neck or Rib
Noisettes
Best End of Neck Roast
Best End Cutlets
French Cutlets
Crown Roast
Guard of Honour

5
Scrag End
Middle Neck Stewing Meat
Middle Neck Cutlets
Scrag End Stewing Meat

6
Shoulder
Roast Shoulder
Rolled and Boned Shoulder
Kebabs

Guard of Honor

This is made from the same pieces of lamb as a Crown Roast. Use two pieces of best end of neck (rack) and turn the roasts skin-side up. Remove 1½ in/3.75 cm (skin only) from the thin ends of the roast. Scrape the exposed bones very cleanly. Stand the roasts on their thick ends, skin side out and push them together so that the exposed bones cross alternately. Skewer the joints firmly together at the base and stuff the center cavity. Protect the exposed bones with a piece of foil, and roast for 1½ hours.

Saddle of Lamb

This can be a big roast weighing from 9-12 lb/4.5-6 kg), and is often prepared with the tail split and curled up and decorated with the kidneys. Score the fat lightly into diamonds and insert slivers of garlic or tiny sprigs of rosemary. Rub with salt and pepper and remove the kidneys which will harden during roasting. Roast it skin-side down for 1½ hours at 375°F/190°C/Gas Mark 5, then turn skin-side up for 1 hour longer. For the last 30 minutes, sprinkle with a little flour and salt and pour on ¼ cup/2 oz/50 g melted butter. Put the kidneys round the roast. Baste with a little red wine or port. Use the meat juices as sauce or use them as a basis for gravy. Either carve in slices parallel to the backbone, *or* cut along the backbone, ease the meat away from it, and cut into chop-like slices at a slight angle following the bones.

Stuffed Crown of Lamb

A Crown Roast of lamb looks so impressive that it is hard to believe it could be so simple to prepare. A crown is made from a pair of best ends (racks) of lamb, 12-14 chops in all. First remove any outside skin and then with a very sharp knife score a line – but do not cut through – several inches from the ends of the bones and trim the meat away from the bones up to the scored line. These trimmed bones will form the top of the crown. The next stage is to shape the base of the crown – simply turn each end of lamb the other way round and cut through the gristle that joins the chops. Use a strong knife and cut in as little as possible – just sufficient to be able to bend the chops round so that they can form a circle. Bend both pieces with the fat side inwards to make a crown and secure firmly with string or skewers.

Stuffing

2 tablespoons butter
1 onion
1 green pepper
3 celery sticks
1 cup/4 oz/100 g fresh white breadcrumbs
1 egg
1 teaspoon prepared mustard

Melt butter in a pan and toss the chopped onion until transparent. Add the chopped pepper and chopped celery and cook for a few minutes. Add the breadcrumbs. Beat the egg with the mustard and bind the mixture. Spoon the stuffing into the center of the crown and cover with a round of foil. Cover the tips of the bones with foil so that they will not burn. Roast at 350°F/180°C/Gas Mark 4 allowing 30 minutes per lb/450 g and 30 minutes over.

Remove the foil and cover the ends of the bones with cutlet frills, small tomatoes or button onions. Sprinkle a little chopped parsley over the stuffing. Allow 2/3 chops per person.

Royal Roast Lamb

3 lb/1.5 kg shoulder of lamb (boned)
Juice of 1 orange
Juice of ½ lemon
2 tablespoons melted butter
1 cup/2 oz/50 g chopped celery
¼ cup/1 oz/25 g chopped almonds
¼ cup/1 oz/25 g chopped mint
Salt and pepper

Combine the orange juice, lemon juice, melted butter and salt. Cook for 5 minutes and mix well. Brush the lamb with the juice mixture and roast at 350°F/180°C/Gas Mark 4, allowing 25-30 minutes per lb/450 g. Brush occasionally with juice mixture during roasting period. Meanwhile combine remaining juice mixture and celery. Cook for 5 minutes. Add mint and shredded almonds. Mix well and serve with lamb.

Orange Roast Lamb

4 lb / 2 kg leg of lamb
1 garlic clove
Cooking oil
¼ cup / 1 oz / 25 g plain (all-purpose) flour
Salt and pepper
½ cup / ¼ pint / 125 ml orange juice
3 tablespoons sugar (demerara if possible)
1 orange

Make small incisions in the leg of lamb, and insert slivers of garlic. Brush the skin with oil, then dust with seasoned flour. Place roast in a roasting pan and cook at 350°F / 180°C / Gas Mark 4 allowing 25–30 minutes per lb / 450 g. When half cooked, sprinkle the meat with half the orange juice. Add the remaining juice 10 minutes later. Ten minutes before the end of cooking time sprinkle the meat with the sugar. Serve, garnished with thin orange slices.

Tomato Stuffed Lamb

Illustrated on pages 96 / 97

2 large breasts of lamb
(about 3–4 lb / 1.5–2 kg in total)
2 onions
3 tablespoons oil
2 large tomatoes
1 large orange
1½ cups / 6 oz / 150 g breadcrumbs
2 teaspoons sage
Salt and pepper
4 tomatoes

Bone the lamb breasts but do not chop them. Chop the onions and cook in the oil until soft. Drain and mix with skinned and chopped tomatoes. Peel the orange and chop the segments. Add to the tomato mixture with the breadcrumbs, sage, salt and pepper. Halve the mixture, and spread one half over both breasts of lamb. Roll and tie with string, and roast at 350°F / 180°C / Gas Mark 4 for 1 hour. Cut the remaining tomatoes in half and fill with the remaining stuffing. Add a little butter and put into the oven with the meat. Continue cooking for 30 minutes.

Lamb in a Tweed Jacket

4 lb / 2 kg leg of lamb
1 garlic clove
¾ cup / 3 oz / 75 g soft white breadcrumbs
3 tablespoons chopped parsley
1 level teaspoon mixed herbs
3 tablespoons butter
1 tablespoon prepared mustard
Lemon juice

Trim the joint and remove as much fat as possible from the top. Cut the garlic clove into small slivers. Make several small, deep incisions all over the lamb and put a sliver of garlic into each.

Place the breadcrumbs, parsley and mixed herbs in a bowl. Melt the butter in a small pan, stir in the mustard and pour on to the other ingredients. Mix together and spread all over the top and sides of the joint, pressing down well with the hands. Sprinkle liberally with lemon juice and leave for 2 hours before cooking. Roast at 375°F / 190°C / Gas Mark 5 for 1½ hours.

Fruit and Nut Stuffed Lamb

3 lb / 1.5 kg shoulder of lamb (boned)
2 tablespoons long-grain rice
¼ cup / 1 oz / 25 g walnuts
¼ cup / 1 oz / 25 g raisins
1 tablespoon sugar (demerara if available)
1 onion
1 pineapple ring
1 teaspoon lemon juice
1 garlic clove

Cook rice in boiling salted water for 9 minutes and drain. Chop walnuts, raisins, onion and pineapple. Combine all the remaining ingredients. Stuff the prepared shoulder, roll up and tie securely. Roast at 350°F / 180°C / Gas Mark 4 for 40 minutes per lb / 450 g.

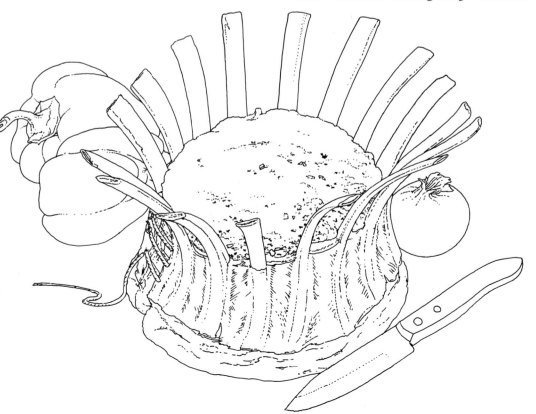

New Zealand Lamb Braid

Recipe on page 106

Lean minced/ground lamb
Onions
Fresh breadcrumbs
Tomato purée
Egg
Worcestershire sauce
Salt and pepper
Puff pastry

Roast Leg of Lamb with Liver and Bacon Stuffing

4 lb/2 kg leg or shoulder of lamb (boned)
1 onion
1 garlic clove
$\frac{1}{4}$ cup/2 oz/50 g butter
6 slices of bacon (streaky)
$\frac{1}{3}$ cup/2 oz/50 g lamb's liver
$\frac{1}{2}$ cup/2 oz/50 g white breadcrumbs
Pinch of sage
Pinch of mint
1 teaspoon parsley
Salt and pepper

Fry the chopped onion and crushed garlic in the butter until soft but not brown. Add the bacon and fry for a further 10 minutes. Add the diced liver and remaining ingredients and mix well. Check the seasoning and use to stuff a boned leg or shoulder of lamb. Roast at 350°F/180°C/Gas Mark 4 for 40 minutes per lb/450 g.

Orange Glazed Lamb Roast

Illustrated on pages 84/85

4 lb/2 kg boned leg or shoulder of lamb

Stuffing
2 tablespoons butter
1 large onion
1$\frac{1}{2}$ cups/6 oz/175 g white breadcrumbs
$\frac{3}{4}$ cup/4 oz/100 g raisins and/or sultanas
$\frac{1}{3}$ cup/2 oz/50 g currants
$\frac{1}{2}$ teaspoon rosemary
$\frac{1}{2}$ teaspoon thyme
Salt and pepper
Grated rind of 2 oranges
Juice of 1 orange

Glaze
$\frac{1}{3}$ cup/2 oz/50 g soft brown sugar
Juice of $\frac{1}{2}$ lemon
Juice of 1 orange
2 tablespoons Worcestershire sauce

Sauce
1 cup/$\frac{1}{2}$ pint/250 ml beef stock
2 teaspoons cornstarch
Salt and pepper

Garnish
2 oranges
Watercress

Melt butter in a pan and fry chopped onion for 3 minutes. Mix with remaining stuffing ingredients and pack into roast of lamb. Secure both ends of roast by tying with string. Place roast in roasting pan. Combine glaze ingredients in a pan and cook gently for 1 minute. Pour glaze over meat and cook at 375°F/190°C/Gas Mark 5 for 2 hours, basting frequently with glaze. To make sauce, blend cornstarch with a little stock and stir into remaining stock. Add glaze left in baking pan and bring slowly to the boil, stirring. Season sauce. Garnish roast with orange slices and watercress and hand sauce around separately.

Australian Honey-Lamb

4 lb/2 kg leg of lamb
$\frac{2}{3}$ cup/8 oz/225 g thick honey
2 tablespoons powdered rosemary
1 garlic clove
Salt and pepper
$\frac{1}{2}$ cup/$\frac{1}{4}$ pint/125 ml white wine or cider

Rub the salt, pepper and rosemary all over the roast, then coat with thick honey. Put a sliver of garlic inside the roast. Put in a roasting pan with 1 cup/$\frac{1}{2}$ pint/250 ml water and wine or cider. Bake at 400°F/200°C/Gas Mark 6 for about 1$\frac{3}{4}$ hours, basting with the water and honey from time to time. Decorate with fresh sprigs of rosemary if available, before serving.

Kosciusko Crust of Lamb

4 lb / 2 kb leg of lamb (boned)

Stuffing
$\frac{1}{4}$ cup / 2 oz / 50 g butter
1 small onion
$\frac{2}{3}$ cup / 2 oz / 50 g mushrooms
Pinch of rosemary
1 teaspoon grated lemon rind
Salt and pepper
1 cup / 2 oz / 50 g fresh breadcrumbs
6 cups / 1$\frac{1}{2}$ lb / 675 g pastry
1 beaten egg

Remove excess fat from the outside of the roast. Melt the butter and cook the finely chopped onion until soft but not brown. Add the chopped mushrooms and continue cooking for a few minutes. Stir in the herbs and seasonings and mix in the breadcrumbs. Stuff this mixture into the bone cavity and tie the joint with string. Place in a roasting pan with the fat on top. Cook at 375°F/ 190°C/ Gas Mark 5 for 1$\frac{1}{2}$ hours. Remove from the oven. Roll out the pastry to fit the roast, place the meat in the center and seal the edges of the pastry. Decorate with pastry leaves and brush with beaten egg. Place on a baking sheet and continue cooking for a further 30 minutes until the pastry is golden brown.

Roast Lamb with Spicy Apricot Glaze

1 whole or half leg of lamb
(3–5 lb / 1.5–2.5 kg)
15 oz / 425 g can of apricot halves
2 teaspoons ground mixed spice
4 cloves
Few drops Worcestershire sauce
Watercress to garnish
Salt and pepper

Season the lamb and roast at 350°F/ 180°C/ Gas Mark 4 for 30–35 minutes per lb / 450 g. Drain the juice from the apricots into a saucepan. Add the cloves, spice and seasoning. Simmer gently until sauce thickens. Thirty minutes before the roast is cooked, cover with the glaze. Baste frequently during the remaining cooking time. Serve garnished with the apricot halves and watercress.

Canberra Stuffed Lamb

4 lb / 2 kg leg of lamb

Stuffing
1 cup / 2 oz / 50 g fresh white breadcrumbs
$\frac{1}{4}$ cup / 1 oz / 25 g walnuts
1 tablespoon uncooked rice
1 teaspoon finely grated orange rind
2 tablespoons finely chopped parsley
$\frac{1}{2}$ teaspoon salt
Good shake of pepper
2 tablespoons brandy
1 egg
Juice of 1 orange

Bone the leg of lamb (bones may be reserved for making of stock or soup). Combine breadcrumbs, walnuts, rice, orange rind, parsley, salt and pepper and bind with the brandy and egg.

Put stuffing into the boned leg and tie with string into a parcel. Transfer to roasting pan, then put into center of oven and cook for 10 minutes at 350°F/ 180°C/ Gas Mark 4. Pour on orange juice then continue to roast for a further 1$\frac{3}{4}$–2 hours, basting at least 3 times during cooking.

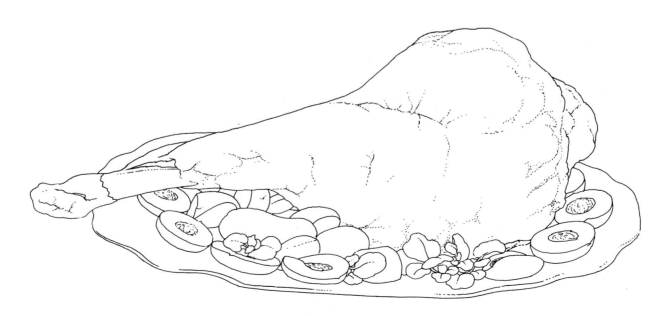

Minted Lamburgers

Recipe on page 86

Minced/ground lamb
Onion
Garlic
Fresh mint
Egg
Oil for frying
Soft buns
Tomatoes
Green salad

Sweet and Sour Lamb

Recipe on page 110

Cooked lamb from leg or shoulder
Can of pineapple cubes
Stock
Carrots
Green peppers
Cornstarch
Brown sugar
Olive oil
Vinegar
Soy sauce

Spanish Stuffed Lamb

3 lb/1.5 kg shoulder of lamb (boned)
Salt and pepper
½ cup/3 oz/75 g cooked rice
12 green stuffed olives
⅔ cup/2 oz/50 g onion
⅓ cup/3 oz/75 g minced (ground) lamb
A little butter
1 garlic clove
Pinch of ground allspice
Parsley
Rosemary
1 egg
2 drops Tabasco sauce
dripping(s)

Gravy
3 tablespoons flour
1 cup/½ pint/250 ml stock
3 tablespoons red wine
1 teaspoon tomato purée
Salt and pepper

Season the surface of the boned lamb with salt and pepper, and crushed rosemary leaves. Season the inside flap and mix together the cooked rice, chopped olives, chopped onion and minced (ground) lamb, softened in butter. Add the seasonings and stir thoroughly. Spread the stuffing inside the cavity and roll up into a cylindrical shape. Tie loops of string at 2-in/5-cm intervals round the roast (spread the dripping[s] over the roast) and place in oven at 400°F/200°C/Gas Mark 6 for 25 minutes per lb/450 g. When the roast is cooked, remove the string and keep hot, and make the gravy using the juices from the roasting pan, add the flour and brown. Pour in the stock, wine, tomato purée and seasoning. Bring to the boil, then simmer and cook for 12 minutes. Pour some over the meat and serve the rest in a gravy boat.

Dill Shoulder

½ shoulder of lamb (2 lb/1 kg)
Salt and pepper
1 bay leaf
Sprig of dill

Sauce
¼ cup/2 oz/50 g butter
½ cup/2 oz/50 g plain (all-purpose) flour
2 cups/1 pint/500 ml stock (from lamb)
3 tablespoons chopped dill
2 tablespoons vinegar
2 teaspoons sugar
Salt and pepper

Place the lamb in a saucepan. Cover with water and add the seasoning and herbs. Bring to the boil, cover and simmer for 1½ hours. Remove shoulder and roast for 30 minutes at 350°F/180°C/Gas Mark 4. Meanwhile prepare the sauce. Melt the butter, add the flour and gradually add the stock. Simmer for 3-4 minutes. Add remaining ingredients and check seasoning. Serve sauce with the shoulder and sprinkle with a little extra dill.

Festival Lamb

4 lb/2 kg boned leg of lamb
¾ cup/4 oz/100 g cooked long-grain rice
1 medium onion
6 slices of lean bacon
4 celery sticks
¼ red pepper
¼ green pepper
Salt and pepper
Pinch of mixed herbs
1 teaspoon ground mixed spice
2 tablespoons cooking oil

Fry the chopped onion and chopped bacon gently in the oil until cooked but not brown. Combine with chopped celery, peppers and seasonings to make the stuffing. Pack the stuffing tightly into the boned leg and tie up both ends of the leg. Roast at 350°F/180°C/Gas Mark 4 for 30-35 minutes per lb/450 g.

Murray Spring Lamb

2 lean lamb breasts (approx. 3 lb/ 1.5 kg)
¾ cup/ 4 oz/ 100 g cooked long-grain rice
1 tablespoon red pepper
2 tablespoons butter
1¼ cups/ 4 oz/ 100 g mushrooms
1 tablespoon French capers
1 egg
Salt and pepper
2 lb/ 1 kg cooked spinach
2 hard-boiled eggs

Bone and trim the breasts, remove the outside skin and place flat, side by side, one breast overlapping the other slightly. Fry gently for 5 minutes in a little butter, the chopped pepper and sliced mushrooms. Mix with the cooked rice, chopped capers and bind together with the egg. Season to taste. Spread the mixture on to the breasts, roll up tightly and secure well with skewers or fine string. Roast the meat at 400°F/ 200°C/ Gas Mark 6 for 1 hour. To serve, cut the rolled breast into slices and place in the middle of a warmed large serving dish. Arrange the hot spinach around the meat and sprinkle very finely chopped egg on top of the spinach.

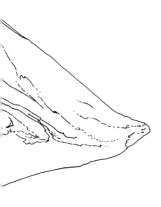

Spring Lamb Roast

2 breasts of lamb (approx. 3 lb/ 1.5 kg)

Stuffing
2 tablespoons butter or margarine
1 medium onion
1 small lemon
2 tablespoons chopped fresh mint
3 cups/ 6 oz/ 175 g fresh white breadcrumbs
1 egg
Salt and pepper

Sauce
½ cup/ ¼ pint/ 125 ml vinegar
1½ tablespoons chopped fresh mint
2 teaspoons fine white sugar
1 tablespoon honey
1 teaspoon soy sauce
1 teaspoon cornstarch
½ cup/ ¼ pint/ 125 ml water

Bone and trim the breasts of lamb. For the stuffing, melt butter in a pan, add finely chopped onion and cook gently for 5 minutes. Grate rind from lemon then discard pith and cut flesh into tiny cubes. Add to remaining stuffing ingredients with onion and mix well. Divide stuffing between breasts of lamb and spread over meat. Roll up and secure with string. Sprinkle with salt and pepper. Place in a roasting pan and cook at 400°F/ 200°C/ Gas Mark 6 for 1 hour until meat is cooked. For the sauce, place all ingredients, except cornstarch and water, in a pan and bring to the boil. Blend cornstarch with water. Stir into sauce, bring to the boil, stirring, and cook for 1 minute. To serve, place lamb on serving plate and remove strings. Pour off excess fat from roasting pan and stir meat juices into sauce. Serve sauce separately with sliced lamb.

Hawaiian Lamb

1 loin of lamb (3 lb/ 1.5 kg)
1 garlic clove
1 tablespoon soy sauce
2 tablespoons sherry or red wine
2 tablespoons honey
1 tablespoon pineapple juice
1 teaspoon ground ginger
Salt
Black pepper
8 oz/ 225 g can of pineapple rings
2 tablespoons butter
1 tablespoon chopped mint

Wipe the roast with a damp cloth. Prepare and finely chop the garlic, and mix with the other ingredients. Put the meat into a casserole and marinate in the sauce mixture for 2 hours. Drain off the marinade, reserving it for later. Roast for 1 hour at 350°F/ 180°C/ Gas Mark 4. Remove the cover and brush the roast with the marinade. Roast for a further 30 minutes. Drain the pineapple rings and fry them lightly with butter. Sprinkle with chopped mint and serve as a garnish for the roast.

Burgundy Lamb

Recipe on page 87

Leg or shoulder of lamb
Bacon
Onion
Garlic
Carrot
Tomato purée
Button mushrooms
Red wine
Salt and pepper
Sugar
Flour
Parsley

Oriental Loin

1 loin of lamb (3 lb / 1.5 kg)
1 tablespoon soy sauce
1 tablespoon apricot jam
2 tablespoons lemon juice
1 garlic clove

Combine the soy sauce, jam, water, lemon juice and crushed garlic. Place lamb in roasting pan, pour over sauce and roast at 350°F / 180°C / Gas Mark 4 for 1½ hours, basting frequently.

Oven Barbecued Lamb Ribs

2 large breasts of lamb (cut into riblets)
4 cups / 2 pints / 1 liter boiling water
2 tablespoons vinegar

Sauce
2 tablespoons soy sauce
2 tablespoons clear honey
2 tablespoons plum jam
1 tablespoon white vinegar
1 teaspoon Worcestershire sauce
1 teaspoon dry mustard
1 teaspoon tomato ketchup
Squeeze of lemon juice

Remove excess skin and fat from the breast ribs. Place in boiling water with vinegar and simmer for 15 minutes. Mix all the sauce ingredients together and heat slowly. Drain lamb, place in a roasting pan and pour over the sauce. Cook at 350°F / 180°C / Gas Mark 4 for 30 minutes then increase to 400°F / 200°C / Gas Mark 6 for a further 20 minutes.

Lamb Scaloppine

Scaloppine is a favorite Italian dish, normally associated with veal. The meat is cut into very thin slices and cooked in a variety of ways. Lamb also makes excellent scaloppine. Cut thin slices from a leg of lamb, slicing from fillet to shank (American to French leg) parallel to the bone. The knife should be very sharp (an electric carving knife is ideal) and the lamb is easier to cut thinly while it is still partially frozen. The slices should then be pounded flat with a wooden mallet or rolling pin.

The lamb scaloppine can then be simply fried in a little butter and oil and served with lemon wedges, or they can be coated in egg and breadcrumbs first, or they can be cooked in one of many sauces.

Lamb Scaloppine with Cheese

1 lb / 450 g lamb sliced thinly from the leg
Four, salt and pepper
1 egg
1 tablespoon water
Fresh white breadcrumbs
2 tablespoons oil
1 cup / 4 oz / 100 g grated Gruyère cheese

Pound the slices of lamb. Dust with seasoned flour. Dip into the egg beaten with the water, then into the breadcrumbs. Brown on both sides in the hot oil. Pour off oil, cover with the grated cheese and place under a hot grill (broiler) until melted and golden.

Lamb Scaloppine Provençal

1 lb / 450 g lamb sliced thinly from the leg
Flour, salt and pepper
1 tablespoon oil
1 onion
1 garlic clove
½ lb / 225 g tomatoes
⅓ cup / 3 fl oz / 75 ml white wine
1½ cups / 4 oz / 100 g mushrooms

Pound the slices of lamb. Dust with seasoned flour. Brown quickly in the hot oil. Add the chopped onion, crushed garlic and skinned and seeded tomatoes. Cover and cook for 15 minutes on a gentle heat. Thicken sauce if necessary, check seasoning and serve on boiled rice.

Lamb Scaloppine à la Crème

1 lb/450 g lamb sliced thinly from the leg
Salt and pepper
2 tablespoons butter
1 small onion
1½ cups/4 oz/100 g mushrooms
⅓ cup/3 fl oz/75 ml white wine
½ cup/¼ pint/125 ml stock
⅓ cup/3 fl oz/75 ml whipping cream
1 teaspoon plain (all-purpose) flour
1 teaspoon butter
Chopped tarragon

Pound the scaloppine. Season and fry them for 3-4 minutes in the butter. Add the chopped onion and sliced mushrooms and cook for a further 5 minutes. Add the wine and stock, reduce by half and strain the sauce. Thicken sauce with the flour and butter and add the cream. Check the seasoning and serve sprinkled with chopped tarragon.

Lamb Scaloppine à la Marsala

2 lb/1 kg lamb sliced thinly from the leg
Flour, salt, pepper, ground ginger
2 tablespoons oil
1 garlic clove
2½ cups/8 oz/225 g mushrooms
½ cup/¼ pint/125 ml marsala or sherry
1 tablespoon tomato purée
Chopped parsley

Pound the slices of lamb. Dust with seasoned flour. Heat the oil in a frying pan with the crushed garlic. Brown the lamb on both sides. Add the sliced mushrooms, cook until browned, and then add the wine and tomato purée. Spoon sauce over the lamb and simmer gently until thickened. Serve on a bed of rice sprinkled with parsley.

Lamb Scaloppine with Lemon

2 lb/1 kg lamb sliced thinly from the leg
Flour, salt and pepper
2 tablespoons oil
8 tablespoons beef stock
1 lemon
4 teaspoons lemon juice
2 tablespoons butter

Pound the slices of lamb. Dust with seasoned flour. Brown quickly in the hot oil, add the stock and place thin lemon slices on top of the scaloppine. Cover and simmer gently for 10-15 minutes. Remove the scaloppine, keep warm. Add the butter to the pan with the lemon juice. Check seasoning and serve garnished with lemon slices.

Lemon and Ginger Chops

4 lamb chump or leg chops

Marinade
4 tablespoons oil
Grated rind of 1 lemon
2 tablespoons lemon juice
1 tablespoon soft brown sugar
1½ teaspoons ground ginger
Salt and pepper

Mix all the marinade ingredients together. Place the chops in a shallow dish and pour the marinade over them. Leave for 2-3 hours, turning occasionally. Remove the chops and place under a hot grill (broiler). Cook for 15 minutes, turning the chops occasionally and basting them with the marinade.

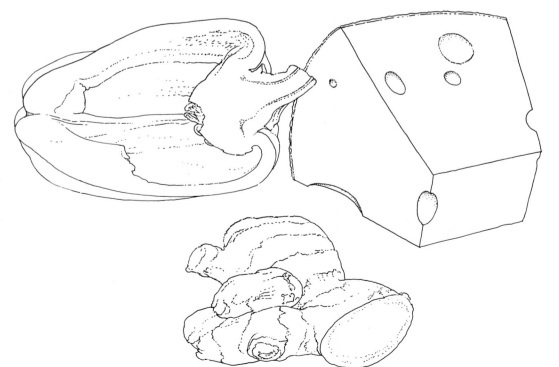

Honeyed Lamb Stew

Recipe on page 111

Best end neck of lamb (rack of lamb)
Onions
Carrots
Can of tomatoes
Clear honey
Oil
Dry mustard

Kebabs with Olives

Recipe on page 42

Steak (rump or round)
Bacon
Tomatoes
Button mushrooms
Stuffed green olives
Oil
Long-grain rice

Barbecue Sauce
Oil
Onion
Flour
Water
Tomato purée
Red currant jelly
Vinegar
Worcestershire sauce
Green pepper

Marinated Lamb Chops

4 lamb loin chops or best end (rack) cutlets
3 tablespoons concentrated curry paste
1 tablespoon lemon juice

Blend the curry paste with the lemon juice and pour over chops or cutlets. Leave overnight. Cook chops over barbecue (or under grill/broiler) for 10–15 minutes turning once. Baste occasionally with the remaining marinade mixture.

Glazed Marmalade Chops

8 lamb chops
2 large cooking apples
$\frac{1}{4}$ cup/2 oz/50 g fine white sugar
$1\frac{1}{2}$ teaspoons ground cinnamon
3 tablespoons butter for frying
2 tablespoons marmalade

Trim away a little fat from the chops if necessary, and grill (broil) for about 10 minutes, turning occasionally. Meanwhile, peel and core the apples and cut into fairly thick rings. Dip them into a mixture of sugar and cinnamon, and fry for a few minutes in butter until soft and beginning to brown. Arrange chops around the sides of the dish and place apple rings in the center. Glaze each chop with a little heated marmalade.

Noisettes Provençales

8 noisettes of lamb
$\frac{1}{4}$ cup/2 oz/50 g butter
1 tablespoon oil

Provençal sauce
$\frac{1}{4}$ cup/2 oz/50 g butter
1 tablespoon oil
1 large onion
1 garlic clove
1 lb/450 g tomatoes
1 tablespoon tomato purée
$\frac{1}{2}$ cup/$\frac{1}{4}$ pint/125 ml dry white wine
Salt and pepper
1 tablespoon chopped parsley

Noisettes are small round thick slices of lamb cut from the loin or rack. They are trimmed of fat, boned and tied into fillets. Each weighs about $\frac{1}{3}$ lb/150 g.

Cook the noisettes in the butter and oil for about 15 minutes, turning occasionally to brown the lamb on both sides. Meanwhile, heat the butter with the oil and add the chopped onion and crushed garlic. Fry gently until soft, but not brown. Stir in the skinned and chopped tomatoes, tomato purée and white wine and bring to the boil, stirring. Allow to cook uncovered over a fairly brisk heat for 10–15 minutes, stirring occasionally. Season to taste with salt and pepper. Sprinkle with parsley and serve with the noisettes.

Spicy Lamb Cutlets

8 lamb cutlets
1 small onion
1 celery stick
1 garlic clove
2 tablespoons butter
2 tablespoons dry mustard
2 tablespoons sugar (demerara if available)
$\frac{1}{2}$ teaspoon Tabasco sauce
2 tablespoons wine vinegar
2 tablespoons Worcestershire sauce
1 bay leaf
Juice of 1 grapefruit
14 oz/400 g can of tomato juice

Fry the finely chopped onion, celery and crushed garlic in the butter for 5 minutes until soft but not brown. Add all the other ingredients and bring to the boil. Simmer for 45 minutes. Remove the bay leaf and check the seasoning. Cutlets should be grilled (broiled) under a hot grill (broiler) for 10 minutes on either side. Serve with the sauce.

Venetian Cutlets

6 lamb cutlets
Pinch of mixed herbs

Sauce
1 medium onion
1 tablespoon oil
8 oz / 225 g can of tomatoes
1 cup / 4 oz / 100 g button mushrooms
1 teaspoon mixed herbs
1 stock cube
6 oz / 175 g spaghetti
$\frac{1}{4}$ cup / 2 oz / 50 g butter

Fry the sliced onion in the oil until soft but not brown. Add remaining sauce ingredients and bring to the boil. Reduce heat, cover and simmer for 15 minutes, stirring occasionally. Meanwhile, cook the spaghetti in plenty of boiling salted water for 10 minutes. Grill (broil) the cutlets for 10–15 minutes, turning once. Drain the spaghetti and toss in melted butter. Place on serving dish and top with the tomato sauce. Place the cutlets on top and sprinkle with mixed herbs.

Greek Style Kebabs

$\frac{1}{2}$ shoulder or $\frac{1}{2}$ leg (2 lb / 1 kg)
(the fillet or American leg end) of lamb
12–16 bay leaves
1 lemon

Marinade
2 tablespoons lemon juice
3 tablespoons oil
$\frac{1}{2}$ teaspoon salt
Pepper
$\frac{1}{2}$ teaspoon mixed herbs

Combine all the marinade ingredients. Cube the lamb and leave in marinade for 2–3 hours. Remove lamb and thread on skewers alternately with bay leaves. Brush with the marinade and grill (broil) for 4–6 minutes, turning occasionally. Serve with lemon wedges, a green salad and French or Greek bread.

Lamb Kebabs with Orange Spice Sauce

$1\frac{1}{2}$ lb / 675 g shoulder of lamb (cubed)
$\frac{1}{2}$ lb / 225 g small onions
Salt and pepper
A little oil

Orange Spice Sauce
1 cup / 6 oz / 175 g soft brown sugar
6 oz / 175 g can
concentrated frozen orange juice
4 tablespoons Worcestershire sauce
Juice of 1 lemon
1 teaspoon prepared mustard
1 tablespoon cornstarch
2 tablespoons water

Thread cubed lamb and onion quarters on to skewers, season and brush with oil. Place over barbecue (or under grill or broiler) and cook for 10–15 minutes, turning occasionally. Blend all the sauce ingredients together and bring to the boil, stirring continuously, and serve with kebabs, boiled rice and a green salad. This simple sauce is also delicious served with loin chops or cutlets.

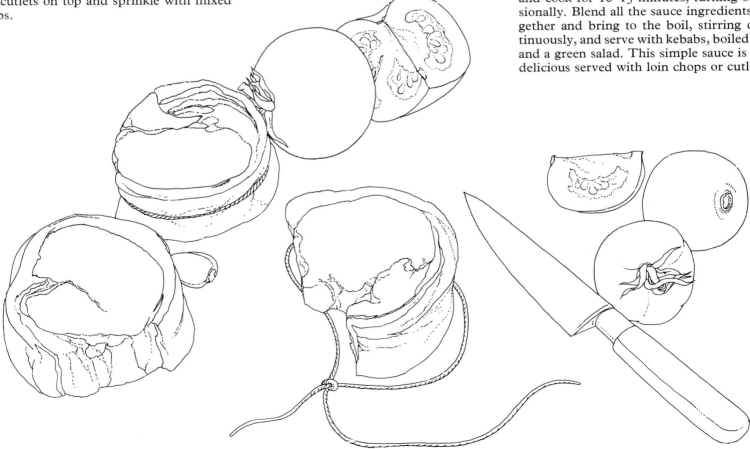

Orange Glazed Lamb Roast

Recipe on page 70

Boned leg or shoulder of lamb

Stuffing
Butter
Onion
White breadcrumbs
Raisins or sultanas
Currants
Rosemary
Thyme
Salt and pepper
Oranges

Glaze
Soft brown sugar
Lemon
Orange
Worcestershire sauce

Sauce
Beef stock
Cornstarch
Salt and pepper

Garnish
Oranges
Watercress

Samosas

Recipe on page 110

Cooked lamb
Curry powder
Onion
Salt and pepper
Chutney
Flour
Suet
Oil

Souvlakia

2 lb/1 kg lamb from leg
2 tablespoons olive oil
Juice of ½ lemon
1 teaspoon marjoram
12 bay leaves
Salt and pepper

Allowing one skewer for each person, cut the lamb into small pieces the size of a walnut and thread on to the skewers with pieces of bay leaf in between. Leave about 1 in/2.5 cm space at either end of the skewers for them to rest on the grill rack. Beat the lemon juice into the olive oil, season with salt, pepper and marjoram and leave the souvlakia to marinate for 30 minutes. Barbecue over a very hot fire, turning constantly, so that the lamb becomes well seared on the outside and tender and juicy inside. Serve straight from the fire with a tomato and cucumber salad and quarters of lemon to squeeze over the meat. The souvlakia may alternatively be cooked under a hot grill (broiler) for about 10 minutes turning occasionally.

Russian Bitkis

1 lb/450 g lean minced (ground) lamb
1½ tablespoons fat
1 onion
4 slices of bread
½ cup/¼ pint/125 ml water for soaking bread
Salt and pepper
Oil for frying
½ cup/¼ pint/125 ml sour cream or yogurt
Tomato sauce (see below)
1 tablespoon chopped parsley

Put lamb in a bowl with the fat, finely chopped onion and parsley. Cut bread in pieces and cover with cold water. Leave to soak through and squeeze dry. Mix with the meat and put ingredients through the mincer. Return to the basin and work thoroughly, adding the water and plenty of seasoning by degrees. When light and short in consistency, shape into cakes on a wet board and fry in hot oil until brown on both sides. Arrange in a fireproof dish, pour a little of the sour cream and tomato sauce over. Bake for 20 minutes at 350°F/180°C/Gas Mark 4. Serve the rest of the tomato sauce separately.

Tomato sauce
1 lb/450 g tomatoes
2 tablespoons butter
1 tablespoon plain (all-purpose) flour
1 cup/8 fl oz/200 ml stock
Sprig of thyme
Sprig of parsley
1 bay leaf
Salt and pepper

Melt half the butter in a saucepan, add the flour. Cook 2-3 minutes and pour on the stock. Cut the tomatoes in two, remove the seeds and excess water and add to pan with the herbs, salt and pepper. Cover and simmer for 30 minutes. Rub through a sieve and add remaining butter.

Minted Lamburgers

Illustrated on pages 72/73

1 lb/450 g minced (ground) lamb
1 onion
1 garlic clove
1 tablespoon chopped fresh mint
½ teaspoon pepper
1 egg
Oil for frying
4 soft buns
4 tomatoes
Green salad

Mix the lamb, finely chopped onion, crushed garlic, mint and seasonings together and bind with the egg. Form into 8 lamburgers and fry for 5-7 minutes each side. Split the buns through the center and toast on the cut side. Place a lamburger on each half of the buns, top with sliced tomatoes and serve with a green salad.

Lamburgers with Blue Cheese Topping

1 lb/450 g
minced (ground) shoulder of lamb
1 large onion
2 tablespoons tomato purée
1 tablespoon Worcestershire sauce
4 tablespoons fresh white breadcrumbs
1 teaspoon mixed herbs
Salt and pepper
Flour for coating
2 tablespoons butter

Blue Cheese Topping
1 cup/4 oz/100 g blue cheese
½ cup/4 oz/100 g butter

Fry chopped onion in butter and mix with all the other ingredients. Shape into 8 burgers on a floured board. Cook over barbecue (or fry or grill or broil) for 7–10 minutes, turning during cooking. Spoon over blue cheese topping before serving. To make this, crumble cheese and mash with a fork. Add butter and blend well. Chill in refrigerator until ready to use. Serve the lamburgers with crusty French bread and a green salad.

Malaysian Lamb Omelette

1 lb/450 g shoulder of lamb
1 onion
2 tablespoons oil
½ teaspoon ground cinnamon
¼ teaspoon ground nutmeg
Salt and pepper
1 cup/½ pint/250 ml water
6 eggs
2¼ cups/12 oz/350 g boiled long-grain rice

Cut the lamb into small cubes or thin strips. Brown lamb in oil and drain off excess fat. Add all the other ingredients except the eggs. Simmer until the mixture is reduced and thick. Allow mixture to cool. Combine cooled meat mixture with beaten eggs and pour into a shallow oiled baking dish. Cook at 325°F/170°C/Gas Mark 3 until the eggs are as firm as desired. Serve with hot buttered rice.

Burgundy Lamb

Illustrated on pages 76/77

1½ lb/675 g leg or shoulder of lamb
6 slices of lean bacon (chopped)
1 medium onion
1 garlic clove
1 medium carrot
1 tablespoon tomato purée
1¼ cups/4 oz/100 g button mushrooms
1½ cups/¾ pint/375 ml red wine
Salt and pepper
1 teaspoon sugar
1 tablespoon plain (all-purpose) flour
1 tablespoon chopped parsley

Fry the bacon in a large deep frying pan until crisp and remove from pan. Fry the sliced onion and crushed garlic in the bacon fat until golden brown. Cut the lamb into 1-in/2.5-cm cubes and add to the onion and carrot. Fry for 10–15 minutes until the meat is brown on all sides. Return the bacon to the pan with the tomato purée, mushrooms, red wine, salt, pepper and sugar, and bring to the boil. Place in a large casserole and bake at 350°F/180°C/Gas Mark 4 for 1½ hours. Beat the flour into 6 tablespoons water and stir into the casserole to thicken.

Sheftalia

1½ lb/675 g minced (ground) lamb
2 onions
4 tomatoes
2 tablespoons chopped parsley
Salt and black pepper

Combine lamb, chopped onions, skinned and chopped tomatoes and parsley together and season well with salt and pepper. Form into sausage shapes. Grill (broil) for about 10 minutes turning until cooked and golden brown.

Lamb Barbecue

Lamb is a delicious meat to barbecue. Seen below are various types of lamb chops and lamb kebabs made of chunks of lamb, green and red sweet peppers, mushrooms, onions and tomatoes.

Almost any barbecue sauce will enhance the flavor of these dishes – try any one of your favorites.

Sauce recipes from the following dishes can be used to baste the chops and the kebabs:

Orange Spice Sauce from *Lamb Kebabs* on page 83;
Marinade from *Greek Style Kebabs* on page 83;
Sauce from *Oven Barbecued Lamb Ribs* on page 78.

Granny's Lamb Stew with Onion Dumplings

3 lb/ 1.5 kg neck of lamb
2 tablespoons/ 1 oz/ 25 g dripping(s)
2 onions
3 large carrots
2 small white turnips or 1 yellow turnip
1 tablespoon plain (all-purpose) flour
2 cups/ 1 pint/ 500 ml water or stock
2 teaspoons thyme
2 tablespoons chopped parsley
Salt and pepper
⅔ cup/ 4 oz/ 100 g frozen peas

Onion Dumplings
¼ cup/ 2 oz/ 50 g butter or margarine
1 large onion
1 egg
1 cup/ 4 oz/ 100 g breadcrumbs
½ cup/ 2 oz/ 50 g
self-raising (self-rising) flour
½ teaspoon salt
Pepper

Heat the dripping(s) in a large pan and fry meat to brown on all sides, then remove from pan. Add sliced onions to pan and cook gently for 5 minutes, then add sliced carrots and turnips and cook for a further 3 minutes. Stir in flour and cook, stirring, until pale golden. Add liquid and bring to the boil, stirring. Add meat, thyme, parsley and seasoning. Cover and simmer gently for 1½ hours, or until lamb is tender. To serve, remove meat from bone, if preferred.

To make the dumplings, melt fat in pan and cook chopped onion gently for 5 minutes until soft but not colored. Beat egg and add butter and onion, breadcrumbs, flour and seasoning. Shape into 8 balls. Add to stew with the peas 20 minutes before the end of cooking time.

Lamb Sukiyaki

½ lb/ 225 g leg of lamb
3 tablespoons stock
4 tablespoons soy sauce
2 tablespoons sugar
1 tablespoon sherry
1¼ cups/ 6 oz/ 175 g long-grain rice
1 tablespoon oil
1 onion
1 leek
3 cups/ 4 oz/ 100 g cabbage (shredded)
1¼ cups/ 4 oz/ 100 g mushrooms
Salt and pepper
2 eggs

Cut the meat into small strips. Combine the stock, soy sauce, sugar and sherry. Cook the rice separately in boiling water for 12 minutes, drain and keep hot. Brown the meat in the oil and add the sliced onion, sliced leek and shredded cabbage. Cook for 3 minutes. Add the sauce and sliced mushrooms and cook for a further 3 minutes. Beat and season the eggs. Add to the meat mixture and continue cooking for 1 minute. Serve with rice.

Lancashire Hotpot

1 lb/ 450 g middle or best end neck of lamb (rack) (cut into cutlets)
1 tablespoon seasoned flour
4 medium onions
2 lamb's kidneys
½ lb/ 225 g carrots
1½ lb/ 675 g potatoes
1½ cups/ ¾ pint/ 375 ml stock

Trim the lamb of any excess fat and coat with seasoned flour. Place layers of meat, sliced onions, sliced kidneys, diced carrots and sliced potatoes in a large casserole, finishing with a layer of potatoes. Add the stock, cover and bake at 350°F/ 180°C/ Gas Mark 4 for 2 hours. Remove the lid and cook for 30 minutes to brown the potatoes.

Lamb and Potato Hotpot

2 lb/1 kg scrag end of lamb (neck of lamb)
1 lb/450 g potatoes
2 large onions
1 thin leek
Salt and pepper
Water
Grated cheese

Remove the meat from the bone and cut into small pieces. Peel the potatoes and slice thinly. Peel and slice the onions and finely chop the leek. Arrange layers of the meat, onions and potatoes in an ovenproof dish. Sprinkle the chopped leek on the layers of onion and season each layer. Finish with a layer of potatoes. Pour the water on top just to cover and then cover the dish. Cook at 350°F/180°C/Gas Mark 4 for about 1½ hours. Remove the lid for the last half hour to brown the potatoes. Grated cheese can be sprinkled on top for extra flavor when browning the potatoes.

Haricot Lamb

1½ lb/675 g
lamb [middle neck (rack), scrag (neck), or breast]
1 cup/6 oz/175 g haricot beans
2 tablespoons butter
¼ cup/1 oz/25 g plain (all-purpose) flour
2 onions
2 carrots
⅔ cup/2 oz/50 g mushrooms
Salt and pepper
2 beef stock cubes
2 cups/1 pint/500 ml hot water
Chopped parsley

Soak the beans overnight. Peel and slice the vegetables finely. Cut the meat in serving pieces and toss in well-seasoned flour. Melt the butter in a saucepan and brown the meat. Add the onions, carrots and mushrooms and color gently. Drain the haricot beans and add to the stew. Pour in the stock made from beef extract cubes and water. Cover and simmer gently for 1¼ hours. Turn out on to a heated serving dish and sprinkle with chopped parsley.

Hungarian Hotpot

2 lb/1 kg neck (rack) of lamb chops
1 tablespoon oil
1 tablespoon paprika pepper
Salt and pepper
1 lb/450 g onions
1 lb/450 g carrots
1 cup/½ pint/250 ml stock
1¼ cups/8 oz/225 g frozen peas
½ cup/¼ pint/125 ml natural yogurt
1 tablespoon chopped fresh parsley

Brown the lamb chops on either side in the hot oil, then remove and drain. Place the chops in a large saucepan and add the paprika, salt, pepper, chopped onions, chopped carrots and stock. Bring to the boil, cover and simmer for 2 hours. Add the peas for the last 15 minutes' cooking. Check seasoning and serve with swirls of yogurt and parsley.

Traditional Irish Stew

2 lb/1 kg scrag end of lamb (neck of lamb)
1 lb/450 g onions
2 lb/1 kg potatoes
Salt and pepper
3 cups/1½ pints/750 ml water
Parsley

Trim and cut the meat into even-sized pieces. Slice the onions and potatoes. Put the meat into a pan, add the water and season with salt and pepper. Bring to the boil and skim if necessary. Add the onions and half the potatoes. Cover the pan with a lid and simmer the stew gently for about 1½ hours. Add the remaining potatoes and cook for a further 30 minutes. If necessary, add a little more water. When cooked, turn the stew into a dish and sprinkle with chopped parsley.

Pasta Hotpot

Recipe on page 111

Middle neck of lamb/neck slice
Oil
Onions
Flour
Salt and pepper
Water or stock
Orange juice
Mint jelly
Pasta shapes

Australian Lamb Casserole

4 lamb chops
A little seasoned flour
Dripping(s)
2 large onions
2 carrots
1 large cooking apple
Salt and pepper
1 cup/½ pint/250 ml cider
1 lb/450 g potatoes
Melted butter

Trim the chops and dip them in seasoned flour. Melt the dripping(s), then fry the chops quickly on each side until brown. Remove from the pan and soften the sliced onions. Arrange half the onions in a casserole with some sliced carrot. Place the chops on top, cover with apple slices and the rest of the onion and carrot. Season well, pour over the cider, and arrange the thinly sliced potato on top. Cover and cook at 350°F/180°C/Gas Mark 4 for 1½ hours, uncovering for the last half hour. To finish, brush the potatoes with melted butter and flash under the grill (broiler) to brown.

Sweet Pepper Casserole

8 lamb cutlets
1 lb/450 g onions
¼ cup/2 oz/50 g butter
1 tablespoon oil
1 green pepper
8 oz/225 g can of tomatoes
½ teaspoon fine white sugar
1 chicken stock cube
Salt and pepper
Pinch of marjoram
4 new potatoes

Place the cutlets under a hot grill (broiler) for 5 minutes, turning once. Place in a casserole and keep hot. To make the sauce, fry the chopped onions in the butter and oil until transparent. Add the pepper, tomatoes, sugar and the stock cube dissolved in ½ cup/¼ pint/125 ml boiling water. Add to the casserole with the sliced new potatoes and cook at 350°F/180°C/Gas Mark 4 for 30 minutes. Serve with more new potatoes.

Carbonnade of Lamb

1 lb/450 g leg of lamb
2 tablespoons seasoned flour
2 tablespoons butter
3 tablespoons oil
1 lb/450 g onions
1 garlic clove
2 cups/1 pint/500 ml brown ale (beer)
Salt and pepper

Cut the lamb into 1-in/2.5-cm cubes and coat with seasoned flour. Melt the butter with the oil and add sliced onions and crushed garlic. Cover and fry gently for 15–20 minutes, stirring occasionally, until the onions are completely softened. Remove the onions and place in a casserole. Fry the lamb in the remaining fat until brown on all sides. Add to the onions with the brown ale (beer) and a little salt and pepper. Cover, and cook at 350°F/180°C/Gas Mark 4 for 1½ hours.

Lamb and Apple Casserole

2 lb/1 kg middle neck (rack) of lamb
Flour seasoned with salt and pepper
2 tablespoons oil
2 onions
2 carrots
1 celery stick
1 cooking apple
2 cups/1 pint/500 ml stock

Dredge the pieces of meat with seasoned flour and brown gently in oil. Chop onions, carrots, celery and apple. Add chopped vegetables and apple to meat and fry for 5 minutes. Add stock. Bring to the boil and simmer for 1–1½ hours.

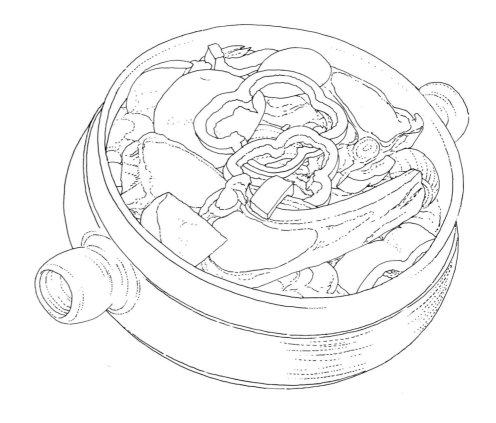

Spicy Lamb Pilaff

1½ lb/675 g shoulder lamb
1 tablespoon cooking oil
2 large onions
2 tablespoons plain (all-purpose) flour
½ cup/¼ pint/125 ml beef stock
1 tablespoon tomato purée
½ teaspoon rosemary
1 tablespoon Worcestershire sauce
Salt and pepper

Pilaff
½ cup/2 oz/50 g butter
1 onion
1¼ cups/6 oz/175 g long-grain rice
2 cups/1 pint/500 ml beef stock
⅓ cup/2 oz/50 g frozen peas
⅓ cup/2 oz/50 g raisins
⅓ cup/2 oz/50 g peanuts
Salt and pepper

Heat oil in pan and fry chopped onions gently for 5 minutes. Add cubed lamb and fry, turning to seal all sides for about 5 minutes. Stir in flour and cook, stirring, for 2 minutes. Blend in stock and tomato purée and bring to boil, stirring. Add rosemary, Worcestershire sauce and seasoning, cover and simmer gently for 30 minutes until lamb is tender.

For the pilaff, melt butter in pan and fry chopped onion for 5 minutes. Stir in rice and cook for 2 minutes. Add stock and bring to boil, stirring. Simmer, uncovered, for 15 minutes. Add peas and simmer for 10 minutes, adding further stock if required. Stir in raisins and peanuts and season well. Serve lamb on a bed of pilaff.

French Style Roast Lamb

2 best ends of neck (rack) of lamb
⅔ cup/6 fl oz/150 ml red wine
3 garlic cloves
1 teaspoon dried mixed herbs
Butter
5 tablespoons fresh breadcrumbs
2 tablespoons chopped parsley

Butter a roasting pan and place the two lamb roasts, fat side up, in it. Butter a double piece of cooking foil and cover the roasting pan with it. Put the wine in a small saucepan with the whole garlic cloves and the herbs, bring to the boil and then let it boil furiously until it has reduced to just over half. Place the lamb in the oven at 375°F/190°C/Gas Mark 5 and after 15 minutes remove the foil and pour on the wine. Replace the foil and continue cooking for 45 minutes, basting occasionally.

Mix the breadcrumbs and parsley in a bowl together with 2 tablespoons pan juices and season well with salt and pepper. When the lamb is cooked, place on an ovenproof dish, heap the breadcrumb mixture on top of each joint and brown under a very hot, preheated grill. Carve into cutlets to serve. The pan juices can be thickened with a little cornstarch.

Cinnamon Pot Roast of Lamb

½ leg of lamb (2 lb/1 kg)
1 garlic clove
1 tablespoon plain (all-purpose) flour
1 teaspoon cinnamon
Salt and pepper
1 tablespoon oil
½ lb/225 g carrots
½ lb/225 g small onions
1 celery stick
3 cups/1½ pints/750 ml stock or water

Stuffing
1 small onion
1 tablespoon oil
2 tablespoons breadcrumbs
½ cup/4 oz/100 g pork sausagemeat
1 teaspoon rosemary
Salt and pepper
1 egg yolk

Remove the bone from the lamb. To prepare the stuffing, chop the onion and fry in the oil for a few minutes. Add the crumbs, sausagemeat, herbs and seasonings. Bind together with the egg yolk. Spread the stuffing on the meat, then roll up and tie securely with string. Insert slivers of garlic under the skin. Mix together the flour, cinnamon, pepper and salt and rub on to the joint. Heat the oil in a large pan, and brown the roast on all sides. Remove the joint then gently fry the sliced vegetables in the hot oil. Place the roast on top of the vegetables. Add the stock or water. Cover and cook over a moderate heat for about 2–2½ hours. Move the roast occasionally to prevent sticking, adding more liquid if necessary. A heavy cast-iron casserole is the best utensil to use for this dish.

*Tomato Stuffed
Lamb*

Recipe on page 67

Breasts of lamb
Onions
Oil
Tomatoes
Orange
Breadcrumbs
Sage
Salt and pepper

Savory Marrow Rings

½ shoulder of lamb (boned and cubed)
2 tablespoons cooking oil
1 small onion
½ cup/3 oz/75 g long-grain rice
⅔ cup/2 oz/50 g mushrooms
2 tomatoes
1 medium-sized marrow or squash
1 cup/½ pint/250 ml stock or water
Salt and pepper

Lightly fry the lamb in the oil with the finely chopped onion. Add the rice, sliced mushrooms and tomatoes. Reduce the heat and add the stock, a little at a time, allowing it to be absorbed by the rice. Continue simmering until all the stock has been absorbed. Cut four slices from the marrow, about 1½ in/3.75 cm thick. Peel and remove the seeds. Place the sliced marrow flat in a casserole or roasting pan and fill the center of each slice with the savory mixture. Cover, and bake at 350°F/180°C/Gas Mark 4 for 1 hour. Serve with brown gravy or hot tomato sauce.

Lamb Curry (Gosht Ki Curry)

2 lb/1 kg shoulder of lamb
1 onion
1 garlic clove
⅓ cup/1 oz/25 g desiccated coconut
2 tablespoons coriander
4 green chillies
1 teaspoon turmeric
3 tablespoons natural yogurt
3 tablespoons oil
1 teaspoon ground ginger
1 tablespoon sesame seeds
1½ cups/¾ pint/375 ml stock
Salt
⅓ cup/2 oz/50 g cashew nuts

Cube the meat, and chop the chillies, removing the seeds. Mix chopped onion and next six ingredients to a paste. Heat oil in a saucepan, add the meat and sprinkle with ginger. Fry until meat is lightly browned on all sides. Add the paste and cook for 10 minutes. Add the sesame seeds. Pour over stock, add salt, stir well. Bring to the boil, and then turn down to a gentle simmer. Cook curry covered for the first half of the cooking time, and then remove lid to reduce the liquid. The finished curry should be quite dry. Put curry onto serving dish and sprinkle with the nuts. Serve with either boiled or fried rice.

Blue Mountain Lamb

3 lb/1.5 kg shoulder of lamb (boned)
3 large onions
1¼ cups/4 oz/100 g mushrooms
3 carrots
2 tomatoes
2 tablespoons butter
Sprig of thyme
Sprig of parsley
1 bay leaf
⅜ cup/3 fl oz/75 ml dry white wine
Salt and pepper

Marinade
¾ cup/6 fl oz/150 ml dry white wine
⅜ cup/3 fl oz/75 ml olive oil
1 onion
3 cloves

Make the marinade by mixing together wine, oil, finely chopped onions and cloves. Cut the boned shoulder into 4 portions. Place the meat into a large mixing bowl and pour the marinade over it. Leave to stand overnight, for at least 4 hours. Peel and quarter the onions, wash and slice the mushrooms, peel and cut the carrots into small cubes and peel and slice the tomatoes. Melt butter in a large thick-bottomed stewing pan and cook all the vegetables gently for 10 minutes, stirring from time to time. Add the meat, well drained, to the vegetables, with the herbs, wine, salt and pepper and (if liked) a crushed garlic clove. Cover the pan tightly and simmer gently on a very low heat for at least 3 hours. Check the amount of liquid from time to time and add a little hot water if necessary. Serve with plain boiled rice or creamed potatoes.

Indonesian Lamb Sateh

1 lb / 450 g shoulder lamb *or*
8 best end (rack) cutlets
3 tablespoons oil
1 large onion
2 garlic cloves
1 tablespoon chopped parsley
2 tablespoons tomato purée
3 cups / 1¼ pints / 625 ml water
3 tablespoons smooth peanut butter
Salt and pepper
Pinch of thyme
1½ cups / 8 oz / 225 g cooked long-grain rice

Cut lamb into 1-in / 2.5-cm cubes and fry in oil for 2 or 3 minutes. Add chopped onion, crushed garlic, parsley, tomato purée, salt, pepper and thyme. Stir in 1½ cups / ¾ pint / 375 ml water and mix well. Dilute peanut butter with remaining water and add to mixture. Simmer gently for approximately 1 hour until lamb is cooked. Check seasoning, and pour over a bed of boiled rice.

Italian Ragoût of Lamb

3 lb / 1.5 kg shoulder of lamb (boned)
2 tablespoons butter
3 oz / 75 g canned anchovy fillets
1 garlic clove
1 teaspoon grated lemon rind
2 teaspoons chopped parsley
¼ cup / 1 oz / 25 g plain (all-purpose) flour
1 beef stock cube
1 cup / ½ pint / 250 ml hot water
Salt and pepper

Cut the lamb into 2-in / 5-cm pieces and brown the meat in the melted butter. Drain off the fat and combine with the anchovies, salt and pepper, crushed garlic and chopped parsley. Add to the pan and dredge with the flour. Stir in the hot stock made with beef cube and water and bring to the boil, stirring until thickened. Cover with a well-fitting lid, and simmer on top of the stove for 1¼ hours, or cook in the oven at 325°F / 170°C / Gas Mark 3. Serve with a purée of potatoes and a sharp-flavored tomato salad.

Dolmades

½ lb / 225 g minced (ground) lamb
3 dozen vine leaves *or* 1 cabbage *or*
1 lettuce
1 large onion
1 teaspoon dried mint
1 tablespoon chopped parsley
Salt and pepper
½ teaspoon ground mixed spice
Juice of ½ lemon
Stock

Sauce
2 tablespoons butter
1 tablespoon plain (all-purpose) flour
1 egg
Juice of ½ lemon

Choose the small, pale green leaves from cabbage or lettuce if used and blanch for 3 minutes in boiling, salted water. Drain well. Fry the chopped onion in a little oil until soft, add the meat and cook gently for 10 minutes. Add herbs, seasoning, spice and rice. Mix well, and put some stuffing on the inside of each leaf. Fold in the sides of the leaf and roll up to make a small parcel. Squeeze gently to keep it together and pack the stuffed leaves close together in a saucepan. Pour the lemon juice over them, and add enough stock to come halfway up the leaves. Put a plate on top, to stop them moving about, cover the saucepan, and simmer for about 40 minutes. Remove. To make the sauce, melt the butter in a saucepan, add the flour, and stir in the remaining stock, with a little water if necessary. Beat the egg with the lemon juice, and stir into the sauce. Pour over the dolmades and serve immediately.

Skewered Sausage Meatballs

Recipe on page 150

Pork sausages
Sage and onion stuffing mix
Salt and pepper
Button mushrooms
Red pepper
Bay leaves
Oil
Beer

Sauce
Can of tomatoes
Tomato paste
Worcestershire sauce
French mustard

Philippino Lamb

1½ lb/675 g lamb (cubed from shoulder)
½ lb/225 g belly (flank) pork
½ cup/¼ pint/125 ml vinegar
2 garlic cloves
2 tablespoons soy sauce
1 tablespoon oil
Salt and pepper
2¼ cups/12 oz/350 g boiled long-grain rice

Cut pork into neat cubes after removing bones. Fry lamb and pork pieces in oil until lightly brown. Add the vinegar, crushed garlic, soy sauce, salt and pepper to saucepan and bring to the boil. Simmer for 45 minutes until meat is tender. A little stock may be required to moisten this sauce. Check the seasoning and pour over a bed of boiled rice.

Simple Meat Loaf

1 lb/450 g minced (ground) lamb
10–12 slices of lean bacon
1 cup/2 oz/50 g fresh breadcrumbs
1 egg
1 teaspoon Tabasco sauce
1 teaspoon mustard powder
Pinch of marjoram
Salt and pepper

Line a 1 lb/450 g loaf pan with the bacon. Blend remaining ingredients in a bowl. Pack into loaf pan. Bake at 350°F/180°C/Gas Mark 4 for 1 hour. Serve hot or cold.

Moussaka

1 lb/450 g minced (ground) lamb
1 lb/450 g aubergines (eggplants)
Oil for frying
2 large onions
1 garlic clove
15 oz/425 g canned tomatoes
2 tablespoons tomato purée
Salt and pepper
2 eggs
½ cup/¼ pint/125 ml cream
½ cup/2 oz/50 g Cheddar cheese
¼ cup/1 oz/25 g Parmesan cheese

Fry the thinly sliced aubergines in oil for 3–4 minutes; remove and drain well. Fry the sliced onions and chopped garlic in 1 tablespoon oil until pale golden brown. Add the minced (ground) lamb and cook for about 10 minutes, stirring occasionally. Add the tomatoes and tomato purée and mix well. Bring to the boil and simmer for 20–25 minutes. Season with salt and pepper. Arrange alternate layers of aubergines and the lamb mixture in a large soufflé dish or shallow casserole. Bake at 350°F/180°C/Gas Mark 4 for 35–40 minutes. Meanwhile, beat eggs and cream together and stir in the cheese. Pour on to the moussaka and return to the oven for a further 15–20 minutes until the topping is firm, well risen and golden brown.

Crusty Lamb Cutlets

6 lamb chops
1 tablespoon oil
2 tablespoons butter
1 small onion
1¾ cups/6 oz/175 g mushrooms
2 (8 oz/225 g) cans of red pimentos
2 tablespoons finely chopped parsley
French mustard
2 cups/8 oz/225 g pastry
Beaten egg to glaze

Trim the chops of any excess fat. Heat the oil and butter and brown the chops briskly on both sides. Leave on a plate to cool. Soften the chopped onion in the pan, add the mushrooms and cook for several minutes. Add the chopped pimentos and parsley and season to taste with salt and pepper. Leave in a bowl to cool. Roll out the pastry thinly and cut out 12 circles – slightly larger than the chops. Spread each chop generously with mustard and with the mushroom and onion and press well down. Place each chop on a pastry circle and place another circle on top, leaving the bone out. Moisten the edges with water and pinch securely together. Place pastry-wrapped chops on a baking sheet and brush with beaten egg. Bake at 400°F/200°C/Gas Mark 6 for 20 minutes.

Lamb and Apple Parcels

4 lamb cutlets
Salt and pepper
2 eating apples
2 cups/8 oz/225 g puff pastry
Lemon juice
1 egg

Rub the cutlets with salt and pepper. Peel and slice the apples and toss in lemon juice. Roll out the pastry into a square and cut into four triangles. Place one cutlet on each of the triangles and divide apple between the four. Dampen the edges and seal up, leaving the cutlet bone protruding, and cover this with kitchen foil. Glaze the pastry with the beaten egg. Place on a baking sheet and bake at 425°F/220°C/Gas Mark 7 for 15 minutes, then reduce heat to 350°F/180°C/Gas Mark 4 for a further 35 minutes. Serve hot or cold.

Lamb and Kidney Pudding

1 lb/450 g leg or shoulder of lamb
½ lb/225 g lamb kidney
1 large onion
2 tablespoons oil
1¼ cups/4 oz/100 g mushrooms
1 cup/½ pint/250 ml stock
Salt and pepper
2 tablespoons plain (all-purpose) flour
Few drops of gravy browning
2 cups/8 oz/225 g
self-raising (self-rising) flour
½ teaspoon salt
1 cup/4 oz/100 g shredded suet
¼ cup/½ pint/250 ml water

Fry the sliced onion gently in the oil until soft but not brown. Cut the lamb into 1-in/2.5-cm cubes and add to the onion with the chopped kidney. Fry for a further 5 minutes, stirring occasionally. Add the mushrooms, stock and a little salt and pepper. Bring to the boil and simmer, covered, for 30 minutes.

Meanwhile, make the pastry. Sift the flour and salt into a large bowl and add the suet. Mix to a soft dough with the water. Roll out three-quarters of the pastry and use to line a buttered 3 pint/1.5 liter pudding basin (steaming mold). Drain the lamb and kidney mixture, reserving the stock. Place the meat mixture in the lined steaming mold. Beat the flour into ½ cup/¼ pint/125 ml cold water and add to the reserved stock with the gravy browning. Bring to the boil, stirring constantly, and cook for 3 minutes. Add ½ cup/¼ pint/125 ml gravy to the lamb and kidney mixture in the dish and reserve the remainder to serve with the pudding. Roll out the reserved pastry to a circle and place on top of the lamb pudding, pinching the edges of the pastry together to seal. Cover with foil and steam for 3 hours.

Lamb Cobbler

2 lb/1 kg scrag end or neck of lamb
2 medium onions
3 tomatoes
1¼ cups/4 oz/100 g mushrooms
1 tablespoon fat
¼ cup/1 oz/25 g plain (all-purpose) flour
1½ cups/¾ pint/375 ml stock
Salt and pepper

Cobbler Topping
2 cups/8 oz/225 g plain (all-purpose) flour
1 teaspoon baking soda
2 teaspoons cream of tartar
½ teaspoon mixed herbs
¼ cup/2 oz/50 g margarine
½ cup/¼ pint/125 ml milk

Cut and trim the lamb. Slice onions, tomatoes and mushrooms. Melt the fat and fry the onions and meat until lightly browned. Put meat, onions, tomatoes and mushrooms in layers into a casserole. Add the flour to the melted fat and cook for a few minutes. Add the stock and seasonings, bring to the boil and pour over the meat. Cook at 400°F/200°C/Gas Mark 6 for 1 hour. Meanwhile, make the topping. Mix all dry ingredients together and rub in the fat. Just before the meat is cooked add the milk to the dry ingredients and mix to a soft dough. Roll out and cut into small rounds. Place on top of the meat and cook for a further 20 minutes.

Cider Sausage Hotpot

Recipe on page 143

Pork sausages
Red cabbage
Onion
Red-skinned apples
Juniper berries
Cider
Red currant jelly
Vinegar
Salt and pepper

Spiced Orange Slices
Oranges
Water
Sugar
Ground cinnamon

Sausage and Potato Loaf

Recipe on page 147

Mashed potato
Sage and onion stuffing
Salt and pepper
Pork sausages
Hard-boiled eggs
Tomato
Grated cheese

Cider, Apple and Lamb Pie

½ shoulder of lamb (boned and cubed)
1 tablespoon oil
1 large onion
2 large cooking apples
1 cup/ ½ pint/ 250 ml cider
Salt and pepper
1 tablespoon cornstarch
2 cups/ 8 oz/ 225 g puff pastry
Beaten egg to glaze

Fry cubed lamb in oil with sliced onion for about 5 minutes until lightly browned. Stir in sliced apples, cider and seasonings. Bring to the boil and allow to simmer gently for about 20 minutes. Add cornstarch dissolved in a little water and cook for a further 5 minutes. Pour into pie pan. Roll out pastry slightly longer than dish. Cut a strip of pastry approximately 1 in/ 2.5 cm around circumference and place on lip of pie pan. Brush with a little water. Place whole piece of pastry on top and seal. Press up the edge of the pastry with the back of a knife. Brush surface of pastry with a little beaten egg. Bake at 400°F/ 200°C/ Gas Mark 6 for 20–25 minutes, until pastry is crisp and golden.

Lamb and Onion Pie

¾ lb/ 350 g cold cooked lamb
½ lb/ 225 g cooking apples
2 tablespoons lard
½ lb/ 225 g onion
½ cup/ 2 oz/ 50 g plain (all-purpose) flour
1 cup/ ½ pint/ 250 ml stock or water
½ teaspoon salt
3 cups/ 12 oz/ 350 g pastry

Line base of a 2-pint/ 1-liter heatproof dish with sliced apples, then cover with chopped lamb. Melt the lard in a pan, add chopped onions and fry gently till soft and pale brown. Stir in flour, cook for 1 minute then remove from heat. Gradually add stock, season with salt, then reheat, stirring, till sauce comes to the boil and thickens. Pour sauce over lamb and apples and leave until cool. Cover pie with pastry, then bake toward the top of the oven at 425°F/ 220°C/ Gas Mark 7 for 20 minutes, then at 350°F/ 180°C/ Gas Mark 4 for a further 20 minutes.

New Zealand Lamb Braid

Illustrated on pages 68/69

¾ lb/ 350 g lean minced (ground) lamb
2 onions
½ cup/ 1 oz/ 25 g fresh breadcrumbs
1 tablespoon tomato purée
1 egg
1 tablespoon Worcestershire sauce
Salt and pepper
3 cups/ 12 oz/ 350 g puff pastry
Beaten egg to glaze

Mix meat, diced onion, breadcrumbs and tomato purée together. Bind with beaten egg and season well. Roll pastry to a long strip approximately 12 × 6 in (30 × 15 cm). Place lamb mixture along the center. Cut strips of pastry toward filling, then braid them over the top. Bend to form a crescent shape. Brush with beaten egg and bake at 425°F/ 220°C/ Gas Mark 7 for 15 minutes then reduce heat to 350°F/ 180°C/ Gas Mark 4 for 30 minutes.

Terrine of Lamb

1 lb/450 g minced (ground) lamb
10–12 slices of bacon
Salt and black pepper
2 teaspoons Tabasco sauce
¼ teaspoon marjoram
1 teaspoon dry mustard
1 teaspoon clear honey
1 cup/2 oz/50 g fresh white breadcrumbs
1 egg
1 onion
1 garlic clove
⅔ cup/2 oz/50 g mushrooms

Line a 1 lb/450 g loaf pan with bacon slices. Chop the onion and mushrooms and crush the garlic. Blend all the ingredients together in a bowl. Pack the mixture into the loaf pan. Bake at 350°F/180°C/Gas Mark 4 for 1 hour. Serve either hot or cold.

Devilled Lamb Pâté

½ lb/225 g cooked lamb (finely ground)
1 tablespoon butter or margarine
1 tablespoon finely chopped onion
1 teaspoon plain (all-purpose) flour
4 tablespoons stock or water
1 teaspoon curry powder
¼ teaspoon dry mustard
Pinch of mixed herbs
Salt and pepper

Melt the butter or margarine over gentle heat. Add the onion and cook until softened but not brown. Stir in the flour smoothly, then add the stock or water and stir until boiling. Draw off the heat and stir in the lamb and the remaining ingredients. Mix thoroughly and check the seasoning. Pack tightly into a small dish or basin and leave to get quite cold. This pâté may be served from the dish, cut into wedges, or turned out and cut into slices or wedges.

Curried Shepherd's Pie

1 lb/450 g cooked lamb (cubed)
1 tablespoon oil
1 onion
1¼ cups/4 oz/100 g mushrooms
1 tablespoon curry powder
1 tablespoon tomato purée
1 cup/½ pint/250 ml stock
Salt and pepper
1½ lb/675 g cooked potatoes

Fry minced or cubed lamb in oil with the chopped onion for 3–4 minutes. Add curry powder and fry for a further 3 minutes. Stir in tomato purée, stock, sliced mushrooms and seasoning. Allow to simmer for about 15 minutes. Pile into a shallow ovenproof dish and top with cooked mashed potatoes. Bake at 350°F/180°C/Gas Mark 4 for 25–30 minutes.

Lamb and Liver Country Terrine

1½ lb/675 g
shoulder lamb (minced/ground)
10 oz/300 g
lamb's liver (minced/ground)
16 slices of lean bacon
1 large onion
1 garlic clove
1 tablespoon tomato purée
1 teaspoon sage
1 teaspoon rosemary
Salt and pepper
½ cup/4 oz/100 g butter
½ cup/¼ pint/125 ml dry red wine
Aspic glaze and orange slices for decoration (optional)

Use the bacon, stretched with a palette knife, to line an ovenware dish. Mix all the other ingredients together and pile in the prepared dish. Fold bacon over the top, then cover with foil. Bake at 350°F/180°C/Gas Mark 4 for 1½ hours. When cooked remove from the oven and press with weights. When cold make an aspic glaze for the top and decorate with orange slices. When top is set, it is ready to serve.

Shepherd's Pie

1 lb/450 g cooked lamb
1 small onion
⅔ cup/2 oz/50 g mushrooms
1 tablespoon dripping(s)
1 cup/½ pint/250 ml gravy
½ teaspoon Worcestershire sauce
1 lb/450 g mashed potatoes
1 egg

Chop or mince the lamb. Fry chopped onion and chopped mushrooms a few minutes in dripping(s). Add lamb, Worcestershire sauce, salt, pepper and gravy. Mix well and turn into an ovenproof dish. Pile mashed potato on top and rough up with a fork. Brush top with beaten egg. Bake at 400°F/200°C/Gas Mark 6 for 40 minutes until browned.

Spanish Barbecued Pork

Recipe on page 115

Thick end of belly (flank) of pork
Butter
Salt and pepper
Sugar
Ground ginger
Mixed spice

Sauce
Worcestershire sauce
Sugar
Malt vinegar
Tomato ketchup
Soy sauce
Garlic
Tabasco sauce
Bay leaves
Stuffed green olives

Lamb Kromeskies

½ lb/225 g cooked lamb (minced/ground)
½ cup/¼ pint/125 ml white sauce
6 slices of lean bacon
2 tablespoons chutney or pickle

Batter
2 cups/8 oz/225 g plain (all-purpose) flour
¾ cup/6 fl oz/150 ml water
2 tablespoons oil
2 eggs
Oil for deep frying

Make the batter by mixing flour, water, oil and eggs, and beating well. Prepare the sauce and add the minced lamb and chutney. Season and allow to cool on a plate. Cut the slices of bacon in half, then stretch. Roll small pieces of lamb mixture in bacon. Dip in the batter and fry till golden brown. These can be prepared without the bacon wrappings, if preferred.

Sweet and Sour Lamb

Illustrated on pages 72/73

¾ lb/350 g
cooked lamb (from leg or shoulder)
15 oz/425 g can of pineapple cubes
6 tablespoons stock
2 small carrots
1 small green pepper
1 tablespoon cornstarch
1 tablespoon brown sugar
2 tablespoons olive oil
2 tablespoons vinegar
2 teaspoons soy sauce

Drain pineapple and reserve juice. Simmer sliced vegetables gently in pineapple juice for 5 minutes or until tender. Mix cornstarch, brown sugar, soy sauce, oil and vinegar and add to vegetables with stock. Add meat cut into 1-in/2.5-cm cubes. Add pineapple chunks, heat and serve with boiled rice.

Samosas

Illustrated on pages 84/85

½ lb/225 g cooked lamb
1 small onion
1 teaspoon curry powder
Salt and pepper
1 tablespoon chutney
1½ cups/6 oz/175 g
self-raising (self-rising) flour
1 cup/3 oz/75 g shredded suet
Oil for frying

Fry onion and curry powder in a little oil for about 3–5 minutes. Add finely chopped lamb and cook for 5 minutes. Add seasoning and chutney. Mix well and allow to cool completely. Make up pastry by mixing flour, suet and a little cold water. Roll out pastry and cut into 8 small rounds with a cutter. Place a small amount of cooled mixture in center of pastry, and bring up dampened edges of pastry to seal into a pasty shape. Deep fry in hot oil for approximately 5–10 minutes until pastry is cooked. Serve hot or cold.

Curried Lamb Salad

¾ lb/350 g cooked lamb (cut into strips)
3 tablespoons mayonnaise
1 tablespoon lemon juice
1 tablespoon tomato ketchup
1 teaspoon curry powder
A few drops Worcestershire sauce
4 celery sticks
A few lettuce leaves
1 tomato
2 tablespoons salted peanuts

Mix mayonnaise, lemon juice, tomato ketchup, curry powder and Worcestershire sauce together. Add the strips of lamb. Serve on a bed of lettuce leaves and garnish with sliced tomato and salted peanuts.

Wellington Salad

¾ lb/375 g cooked lamb
1–2 teaspoons orange liqueur (optional)
3 oranges
2 celery sticks
⅔ cup/2 oz/50 g desiccated coconut
1 teaspoon curry powder
4 tablespoons mayonnaise
1 lettuce

Cut the lamb into ½-in/1.25-cm cubes and sprinkle with the liqueur. Cut 3–4 slices from one of the oranges and reserve for decoration. Chop the remaining oranges and add to the lamb with the chopped celery. Mix the coconut, curry powder and mayonnaise together. Add to the lamb mixture and mix well. Arrange the lettuce leaves on a serving plate and pile the salad on top. Garnish with the reserved orange slices.

Honeyed Lamb Stew

Illustrated on page 80

3 lb/1.5 kg best end neck of lamb (rack of lamb)
3 medium onions
6 small carrots
14 oz/400 g can of tomatoes
1 tablespoon clear honey
3 tablespoons cooking oil
1 teaspoon dry mustard

Heat the oil and fry the sliced onions until soft and golden. Rub the lamb with the mustard and season with salt and pepper. Brown in the oil. Add the chopped carrots and drained tomatoes. Put the tomato juice into a measuring jug and stir in the honey. Make up to 1 cup/½ pint/250 ml with hot water. Pour over the meat, bring to the boil, then cover tightly. Cook at 375°F/190°C/Gas Mark 5 for 1½ hours.

Pasta Hotpot

Illustrated on pages 92/93

2 lb/1 kg middle neck of lamb (neck slice)
3 tablespoons oil
2 medium onions
¼ cup/1 oz/25 g plain (all-purpose) flour
Salt and pepper
2 cups/1 pint/500 ml water or stock
½ cup/¼ pint/125 ml orange juice
3 teaspoons mint jelly
¾ cup/4 oz/100 g pasta shapes

Cut the lamb into even-sized pieces and brown on all sides in oil. Remove the lamb to a plate. Slice the onion and fry gently in the remaining oil for 5 minutes. Stir in the flour and cook for 1 minute. Add seasoning and gradually stir in the water or stock and orange juice. Bring to the boil and simmer until lightly thickened. Return the lamb to the pan and stir in the mint jelly. Cover and cook at 300°F/150°C/Gas Mark 2 for 2½ hours. Cook the pasta shapes in boiling salted water until just tender. Drain well and add to the hotpot. Return to the oven for 15 minutes.

PORK *American Cuts*

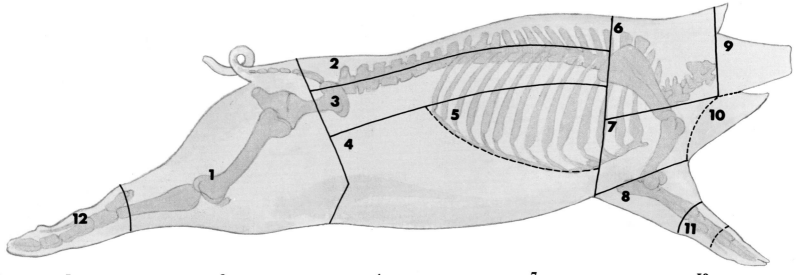

1 **Ham** Ham (Shank Half) Center Ham Slice Fresh Ham Slice Ham (Butt Half) Rolled Fresh Ham Roast **2** **Fat Back**	**3** **Loin** Boneless Loin Roast Canadian Style Bacon Sirloin Roast Blade Loin Roast Crown Roast Loin Chop Loin Roast Butterfly Chop Rib Chop Frenched Rib Chop Tenderloin (Roast or Chop)	**4** **Flank** Bacon Salt Pork **5** **Spareribs** **6** **Shoulder Butt** Blade Steak Boston Butt Rolled Boston Butt Smoked Shoulder Butt	**7** **Picnic Shoulder** Rolled Fresh Picnic Shoulder Smoked Picnic Shoulder Fresh Picnic Shoulder Cushion Picnic Shoulder **8** **Hock** Fresh Shoulder Hock Arm Steak **9** **Snout**	**10** **Jowl** **11** **Forefoot** **12** **Hind Foot**

British Cuts

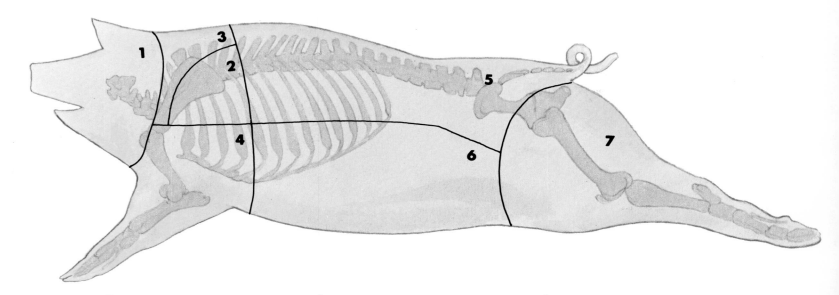

1
Head

2
Blade
Blade Roast
Rolled Blade Roast
Neck End Roast (Chine)
Boned and Rolled Neck End Roasts

3
Spare Rib
Spare Rib Roast
Pork Cutlets

4
Hand and Spring
Hand, Spring or Shoulder Roasts
Rolled Hand, Spring or Shoulder Roast
Stewing Meat

5
Loin
Chump Chops
Escalopes
Loin Chops
Spare Rib Chops
Tenderloin or Fillet
Roast Loin
Crown Roast of Pork

6
Belly
Fresh Belly Pork Roast
Rolled Belly Pork Roast
Salted Belly
Flank Pork
Spare Ribs

7
Leg
Fillet Half Leg Roast
Fillet Half Leg Steaks
Knuckle Roast
Boned Knuckle Roast
Leg Roast

HAM/BACON

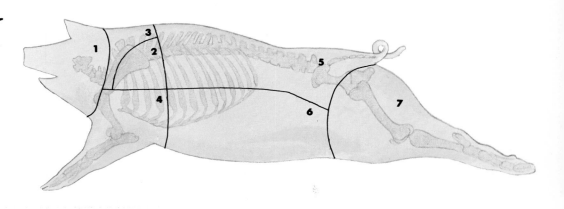

1
Head

2
Collar
Whole Collar
Middle Collar Roast
Prime Collar
End Collar

3
Forehock
Fore Slipper
Small Hock
Butt

4
Back
Top Back Rashers
Middle Cut
Short Back Rashers
Oyster Cut
Long Back Rashers
Bacon Chops

5
Flank
Streaky
Streaky Rashers

6
Gammon
Corner Gammon
Middle Gammon
Hock
Gammon Slipper

Roast Pork Loin with Stuffed Tomatoes

2½ lb/1.25 kg loin of pork
4 tomatoes
4 tablespoons sage and onion stuffing
Salt and pepper

Have the pork chined and scored. Roast the pork at 350°F/180°C/Gas Mark 4 for 30 minutes per lb/450 g and 30 minutes over. Cut the tops off the tomatoes and scoop out the centers. Mix the tomato pulp with the stuffing and fill the tomatoes. Put the tomatoes around the pork for the last 20 minutes' cooking time.

Apricot Pork

3 lb/1.5 kg loin of pork
1 lb/450 g can of apricots (drained)
¼ lb/100 g pork sausagemeat
1½ cups/3 oz/75 g breadcrumbs
Salt and pepper
Lard

Chine the loin and cut a pocket through the fat from side to side. Mash all the apricots except six with the sausagemeat and breadcrumbs. Season well and place this mixture in the pocket in the meat. Brush the scored skin with melted lard and sprinkle liberally with salt. Bake in oven at 375°F/190°C/Gas Mark 5 for 2½ hours. Serve cold, cut into thin slices. The bones can be removed for easy carving.

Stuffed Belly (Flank) of Pork

2 lb/1 kg lean belly (flank) of pork

Stuffing
1 cup/2 oz/50 g white breadcrumbs
¼ cup/1 oz/25 g shredded suet
¼ cup/1 oz/25 g raisins or sultanas
½ teaspoon mixed herbs
1 egg

Sauce
2 tablespoons red currant jelly
½ lb/225 g apple purée

Remove any bones from pork and trim off the excess fat. Score the skin. Make the stuffing by mixing the breadcrumbs, suet, raisins and herbs together and bind with the egg. Spread the stuffing over the pork, roll up and tie securely with string. Wrap the pork in cooking foil and place in a roasting pan in the oven for 30 minutes at 400°F/200°C/Gas Mark 6. Lower the temperature to 350°F/180°C/Gas Mark 5 and continue to cook for a further 1¾ hours. Remove the foil and return to the oven for 15 minutes to brown and crisp the crackling. Make the sauce by melting the red currant jelly and adding the apple purée. Heat through and serve the sauce separately in a gravyboat.

Celebration Pork

4 lb/2 kg loin of pork with skin on
¼ lb/100 g celery
1 medium onion
⅓ cup/2 oz/50 g raisins or sultanas
⅓ cup/2 oz/50 g long-grain rice
1 egg
Salt and pepper
Pinch of ground nutmeg
A little melted lard
Onions
Potatoes

Chine the roast of pork and then remove the backbone. Score the skin. To make the stuffing, mince the celery, onion and raisins together and then add the cooked rice and egg. Add seasonings and mix well together. Place the roast on a board with the skin side downwards. Make a deep incision through the flesh right under the rib bones. Put the stuffing into this cavity and secure with a skewer. Place a piece of foil over the stuffing. Put the roast in a roasting pan with the skin side upwards. Brush with melted lard and sprinkle with salt. Roast at 375°F/190°C/Gas Mark 5 for 2 hours. Add some peeled whole onions and potatoes round the meat about 1 hour before the end of the cooking time.

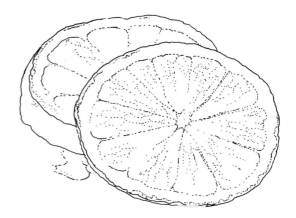

Spanish Barbecued Pork

Illustrated on pages 108/109

3 lb/1.5 kg thick end of belly (flank) of pork
¼ cup/2 oz/50 g butter
½ teaspoon salt
Pepper
1 teaspoon sugar
1 teaspoon ground ginger
1 teaspoon mixed spice

Sauce

1 tablespoon Worcestershire sauce
2 teaspoons sugar
2 tablespoons malt vinegar
8 tablespoons tomato ketchup
2 tablespoons soy sauce
2 garlic cloves
Dash of Tabasco sauce
2 bay leaves
⅔ cup/3 oz/75 g Spanish stuffed green olives

Make sure the skin of the pork is scored. Mix butter, salt, pepper, sugar, ginger and spice and spread all over the meat. Roast uncovered at 400°F/200°C/Gas Mark 6 for 1 hour, basting from time to time. Mix Worcestershire sauce, sugar, vinegar, tomato ketchup, soy sauce, crushed garlic, Tabasco sauce and bay leaves. Drain all fat from the meat. Pour the sauce around the meat and cook for 15 minutes. Add halved olives to sauce just before serving.

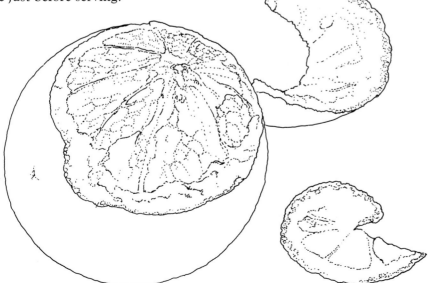

Orange Roast Pork

3 lb/1.5 kg loin of pork
Salt and pepper
3 tablespoons cooking oil or fat
2 oranges
2 tablespoons clear honey

Using a very sharp knife, score the pork rind deeply and evenly into a diamond pattern. Season the roast with salt and pepper and rub the rind with a little oil and plenty of salt, rubbing salt into the cuts. Preheat the oven to 375°F/190°C/Gas Mark 5. Heat remaining oil in the roasting pan and seal the ends of the meat in the hot fat. Mix the grated orange rind, juice and honey together and pour half over the meat. Roast for 1½ hours then increase oven temperature to 425°F/220°C/Gas Mark 7 and pour remaining orange and honey mixture over the meat. Roast for 30 minutes. Serve with some extra orange slices and watercress.

Spiced Pork

1½ lb/675 g loin of pork
Salt
2 tablespoons dripping(s)
¼ cup/1 oz/25 g plain (all-purpose) flour
Pinch of rosemary
½ small onion
1 cup/½ pint/250 ml stock or water
1 cup/½ pint/250 ml vinegar

Rub salt and rosemary into scored pork skin. Roast at 400°F/200°C/Gas Mark 6. Remove meat from roasting pan and keep pork warm. Add dripping(s) to pan juices then mix in the flour and chopped onion, stir and cook for 3 minutes. Add the stock and vinegar, bring to the boil and simmer for 7 minutes. Slice the pork and serve with the vinegar sauce and vegetables.

Stuffed Loin of Pork

3 lb/1.5 kg loin of pork (boned)
1 cup/2 oz/50 g fresh breadcrumbs
1 cooking apple
¼ lb/100 g pork sausagemeat
Salt and pepper
Pinch of rosemary
Melted lard

Score the pork skin deeply and rub it over with melted lard and salt. Cut through the fat under the skin to make a pocket. Mix together breadcrumbs, sausagemeat, finely chopped apple, rosemary and seasoning to make a stuffing. Place this into the pocket. Put meat in a roasting pan and roast at 400°F/200°C/Gas Mark 6 for 20 minutes then at 350°F/180°C/Gas Mark 4 allowing 30 minutes per lb/450 g and 30 minutes over.

Pork Crumble

Recipe on page 118

Lean pork
Leeks
Butter
Flour
Stock
Salt and pepper

Topping
Flour
Salt
Butter
Grated Cheddar cheese

Pork Crumble

Illustrated on pages 116/117

1 lb/450 g lean pork
1 lb/450 g leeks
2 tablespoons butter
¼ cup/50 g plain (all-purpose) flour
2 cups/1 pint/500 ml stock
Salt and pepper

Topping
1 cup/4 oz/100 g plain (all-purpose) flour
Pinch of salt
¼ cup/2 oz/50 g butter
¾ cup/3 oz/75 g grated Cheddar cheese

Cube the pork and slice the leeks into circles. Melt the butter and cook the pork and leeks until just golden. Drain and put the pork and leeks into an ovenproof dish. Work the flour into the remaining fat and cook for 1 minute. Stir in the stock and season well. Simmer and stir until smooth, and then pour over the pork. Cover and cook at 350°F/180°C/Gas Mark 4 for 45 minutes. Stir together the flour and salt and rub in the butter until the mixture is like breadcrumbs. Stir in the grated cheese. Sprinkle on top of the meat and cook without a lid for 45 minutes.

Savory Stuffed Pork

4 lb/2 kg pork shoulder (boned)

Stuffing
1 cup/4 oz/100 g breadcrumbs
3 slices back bacon
1 cooking apple
Salt and pepper
2 tablespoons chopped parsley
1 teaspoon paprika pepper
1 medium onion
1 egg
Stock or milk

Cut a pocket in the meat to hold the stuffing. Dice the bacon, apple and onion. Mix stuffing ingredients, adding beaten egg and stock to bind. Fill the pocket with stuffing and sew up with strong thread. Place roast on a rack in a roasting pan with ½ in/1.25 cm cold water. Bake at 350°F/180°C/Gas Mark 4 for 30 minutes per lb/450 g and 30 minutes over.

Fruited Pork Casserole

1½ lb/675 g lean pork or 4–6 pork chops
½ cup/3 oz/75 g prunes
⅔ cup/3 oz/75 g dried apricots
1½ cups/¾ pint/375 ml cold tea
1 onion
3 tablespoons oil
6 tablespoons plain (all-purpose) flour
Salt and pepper
1 teaspoon ground cinnamon
1 cup/½ pint/250 ml stock
1 cup/½ pint/250 ml beer
½ lb/225 g potatoes

Soak the prunes and apricots overnight in the tea. Slice the onion and fry in the oil for 4 minutes. Toss the cubed pork in the flour seasoned with salt and pepper. Fry until brown on all sides and then stir in remaining flour and cinnamon and cook for 1 minute. Gradually add stock and beer and bring to the boil. Put into a casserole with the drained fruit and sliced potatoes. Cover and cook at 350°F/180°C/Gas Mark 4 for 1½ hours. If preferred, 4–6 pork chops may be used instead of the cubed pork.

Country Pork Bake

4 pork chops
2 tablespoons lard
1 garlic clove
8 juniper berries
1½ lb/675 g potatoes
1 medium onion
Salt and pepper
Pinch of ground nutmeg
6 slices of bacon
4 tablespoons white wine or cider

Cut the garlic into 4 pieces and put a piece of garlic and 2 juniper berries close to the bone of each chop. Brown the chops in the lard on both sides. Slice the potatoes and onions thinly and put half into an ovenproof dish. Season with salt, pepper and nutmeg. Put chops on top and cover with remaining potatoes and onion, seasoning well. Cover with pieces of bacon, and pour in wine or cider. Cover tightly and cook at 300°F/150°C/Gas Mark 2 for 2½ hours. Drain off surplus fat and continue cooking without a lid for 15 minutes to brown the top.

Sweet and Sour Pork Casserole

4 pork chops
Seasoned flour
3 tablespoons oil
½ lb/225 g tiny onions
10 oz/300 g can crushed pineapple
3 tablespoons clear honey
2 tablespoons orange marmalade
4 tablespoons vinegar
1 large carrot
¼ cup/1 oz/25 g split almonds

Coat the chops in seasoned flour and cook in the oil until lightly browned on all sides. Drain and put into a casserole. Peel the onions and keep them whole. Cook in the oil gently for 5 minutes. Add to the chops. Put the pineapple, honey, marmalade, vinegar and grated carrot into the pan. Bring to the boil and simmer for 5 minutes and pour over the chops. Cover and cook at 350°F/180°C/Gas Mark 4 for 2½ hours. Sprinkle with the almonds just before serving.

Mexican Pork

1 lb/450 g lean pork
Seasoned flour
3 tablespoons oil
8 oz/225 g can of pineapple chunks
Chicken stock
1 green pepper
¼ cup/1 oz/25 g raisins
12 oz/350 g can of corn

Cut the pork into thin strips and coat in seasoned flour. Cook in the oil until lightly browned on all sides. Drain the pineapple and make up the juice to 2 cups/1 pint/500 ml with chicken stock. Stir into the pork and add the pineapple chunks, chopped green pepper and raisins. Cover and simmer for 1 hour. Drain the corn and stir into the pan. Simmer for 10 minutes and serve.

Pork Korma

1 lb/450 g lean pork
1 teaspoon ground turmeric
1 garlic clove
1½ cups/¾ pint/375 ml natural yogurt
1 orange
3 tablespoons oil
1 medium onion
Salt
5 cloves
2 cinnamon sticks

Cut the pork into cubes and put into a dish. Cover with turmeric, crushed garlic, yogurt, grated rind and juice of orange, and leave in a cool place for 1 hour. Slice the onion and cook in the oil for 4 minutes. Season with salt and add cloves and 1 crushed cinnamon stick. Fry for 1 minute. Add the meat and covering liquid, cover and simmer for 1 hour. Just before serving, sprinkle with the remaining crushed cinnamon stick.

Pork with Capers

1 lb/450 g pork
1 onion
1 carrot
1 tablespoon capers
⅓ cup/3 fl oz/75 ml red wine
1 bay leaf
Sprig of thyme
Sprig of parsley
Pepper
¼ cup/2 oz/50 g butter
¼ cup/1 oz/25 g plain (all-purpose) flour
½ cup/¼ pint/125 ml beef stock

Chop vegetables. Tie herbs together. Put these ingredients round the meat. Marinate for 8 hours with red wine. Drain and put liquid in casserole. Melt the butter and brown the meat. Stir in flour, blend in marinade and gravy. Season, bring to the boil, cover and simmer for 2 hours. Serve meat in slices and reduce the sauce in casserole. Stir in the capers at the last moment and pour the sauce over the meat.

Somerset Pork with Cider Cream Sauce

Recipe on page 134

Pork fillet (or thin pork steaks)
Flour
Butter
Onion
Mushrooms
Cider
Salt and pepper
Whipping cream
Chopped parsley

Veal Sevillana

Recipe on page 62

Veal escalopes
Butter
Onion
Mushrooms
Stuffed green olives
Fresh white breadcrumbs
Egg
Salt and pepper
Flour
Chicken stock
Orange
Sherry
Cream

Pork and Apple Bake

6 small pork chops
2 pig's kidneys
1½ lb/675 g potatoes
1 lb/450 g onions
1 apple
2 teaspoons sage
Salt
1 tablespoon tomato purée
½ cup/¼ pint/125 ml water

Peel and slice potatoes and onions, and put in layers in a casserole, reserving about 2 potatoes. On top of the layers put the chops and sliced kidneys, and sprinkle each layer of meat with a little chopped apple, sage, salt and tomato purée. Finish with a layer of potatoes, pour in water, cover and bake at 325°F/170°C/Gas Mark 3 for 3 hours.

Pork Chops in Orange Sauce

4 large pork chops
2 tablespoons lard
Flour
Salt and pepper
¼ teaspoon ground nutmeg
1 cup/½ pint/250 ml orange juice
2 teaspoons grated orange rind
1 teaspoon vinegar

Melt lard in heavy saucepan. Dip chops in flour seasoned with salt and pepper, and brown on both sides in hot fat. Put in casserole, add nutmeg, orange juice, rind and vinegar. Cover and cook in moderate oven at 350°F/180°C/Gas Mark 4 for 2 hours.

Southern Pork Casserole

4 large pork chops
1 tablespoon seasoned flour
2 tablespoons lard
4 medium potatoes
1 cooking apple
1 large onion
1 lb/450 g can of tomatoes
2 teaspoons brown sugar
1 tablespoon prepared mustard
1 teaspoon salt

Toss chops in seasoned flour. Brown on both sides in lard. Remove from fat and keep hot. Peel and slice potatoes and apple. Peel and slice onion, and fry till brown in remaining fat. Grease a casserole, and put in a layer of potatoes, then apple. Heat tomatoes with brown sugar, mustard and salt, stir in fried onion and pour over potatoes and apple. Arrange the chops on the top of the dish, cover and cook at 350°F/180°C/Gas Mark 4 for 1½ hours.

Pork and Cranberry Bake

6 small pork chops
Salt
1 lb/450 g cranberries
½ teaspoon powdered cloves
⅓ cup/4 oz/100 g clear honey

Brown chops on both sides, sprinkle with salt, and put three of them in a casserole. Put cranberries through a grinder, and mix with cloves and honey. Spread on chops, and top with the remaining chops, spreading on another layer of the cranberry mixture. Cover and bake at 350°F/180°C/Gas Mark 4 for 1 hour.

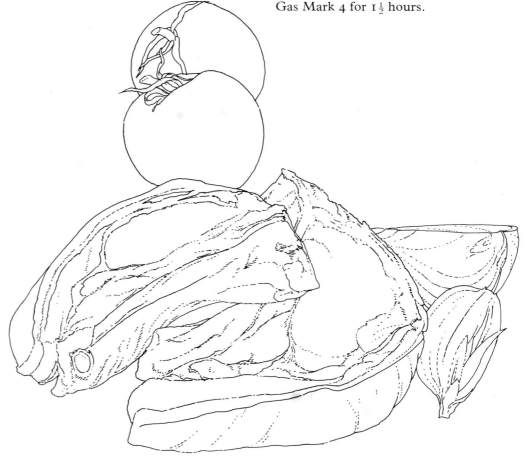

Pork-Pot

1½ lb/675 g
lean pork (from hand, hock or shoulder)
1 large onion
2 carrots
½ cup/¼ pint/125 ml cider
1 bay leaf
Pinch of mixed herbs
Garlic clove
Salt and pepper
2 tablespoons butter
¼ cup/1 oz/25 g plain (all-purpose) flour
2 tablespoons milk

Cube the meat then put it with the cider, chopped onion, sliced carrots, bay leaf, herbs, crushed garlic and seasoning into an ovenproof dish, cover and cook at 325°F/170°C/Gas Mark 3 for 1¾ hours. Drain off pan juices, and keep meat and vegetables warm. Melt the butter in a small saucepan, stir in the flour and cook for 2 or 3 minutes. Add sufficient strained liquid to the milk to make up 1 cup/½ pint/250 ml. Gradually add to the saucepan, stirring, to make a sauce, cook for 3 or 4 minutes, then pour over the pork.

Belly (Flank) of Pork Casserole

1½ lb/675 g pork belly (flank)
1 onion
1 apple
2 tablespoons tomato purée
½ cup/¼ pint/125 ml beef stock
Salt and pepper

Peel and slice onion and apple. Place at the bottom of a casserole. Place the meat on top. Add the stock and tomato purée and pour into the casserole. Season with salt and pepper. Bake at 350°F/180°C/Gas Mark 4 for 2 hours.

Potted Pork

1 lb/450 g hand, shoulder or blade of pork
1 lb/450 g pork sausagemeat
¼ teaspoon garlic salt
¼ teaspoon basil
¼ teaspoon black pepper
¼ teaspoon salt
¼ teaspoon marjoram
Pinch of ground nutmeg
2 cups/1 pint/500 ml water
2 tablespoons gelatine

Cut the pork into very small pieces and put into pan with the sausagemeat, seasonings and water. Bring to boil. Put lid on, reduce heat and simmer for 1 hour. Strain off the liquid and dissolve the gelatine in it. Allow to get cold. Skim off fat and then add liquid to the meat mixture. Put into 2 lb/1 kg loaf pan or dish and allow to set. Serve cut into slices.

Fruit-Stuffed Pork

1 leg of pork (boned)
6 × ½ in/1.25 cm slices white bread
1 cup/½ pint/250 ml stock
2 tablespoons butter
2 celery sticks
½ cup/2 oz/50 g dried apricots
1 lb/450 g cooking apples
⅓ cup/2 oz/50 g raisins
1 teaspoon marjoram
2 tablespoons chopped parsley
Salt and pepper

Cut the crusts off the bread and soak in the stock for 5 minutes, then wring dry in the hands and put into a large bowl. Melt the butter in a pan and fry the finely chopped celery for 5 minutes. Add to the bread, together with the remaining ingredients, mixing thoroughly. Use half the stuffing to stuff the leg of pork and make small balls with remaining mixture. Rub skin of pork with a little oil and sprinkle with salt. Roast at 400°F/200°C/Gas Mark 6 and continue cooking, allowing a total cooking time of 30 minutes per lb/450 g and 30 minutes over. Put the stuffing balls into the roasting pan for the last 30 minutes.

Pork Chops with Cabbage

Recipe on page 127

Pork chops
Cabbage
Salt and pepper
Butter
Onion
Garlic
Cider
Whipping cream
Cheddar cheese

Navarin of Pork

1½ lb/675 g diced pork shoulder
1 cup/6 oz/175 g chopped onions
2 tablespoons bacon fat
A little seasoned flour
2½ cups/1 lb/450 g diced white turnips
1 cup/6 oz/175 g diced carrots
1 cup/6 oz/175 g diced parsnips
1 cup/8 fl oz/200 ml stock
1 teaspoon salt
½ teaspoon pepper
¼ teaspoon ground nutmeg
¼ teaspoon celery salt
1 bay leaf
Chopped parsley

Fry the chopped onion in the bacon fat for a few minutes. Shake the seasoned flour over the pork and add to the onion. Fry for a few minutes more, stirring well. Add the diced turnips, carrots, parsnips and stock. Add seasonings and stir well together. Bring to the boil, reduce heat and put lid on. Simmer slowly for 1¼ hours. Reseason and serve in hot dish sprinkled with parsley.

Pork Goulash

1½ lb/675 g shoulder or hand (hock) of pork
2 onions
2 tomatoes
1 green pepper
⅔ cup/2 oz/50 g mushrooms
Salt and pepper
2 teaspoons paprika
¼ cup/1 oz/25 g plain (all-purpose) flour
1 cup/½ pint/250 ml stock

Put the diced pork, sliced onions, tomatoes, green pepper and mushrooms into a casserole. Season with salt and pepper. Blend the paprika and flour to the stock and pour into the casserole. Cover with lid and cook for 1½ hours at 325°F/170°C/Gas Mark 3.

Pork in Red Wine

1½ lb/675 g slices of pork shoulder
Ground nutmeg
½ cup/¼ pint/125 ml red wine
¼ cup/1 oz/25 g raisins
2 shallots
Salt and pepper

Rub the pork with a little nutmeg and lay in an ovenproof dish. Add all the ingredients and cover with lid. Simmer slowly for 1 hour. Put meat on a hot dish and make the liquid into a rich gravy by thickening it with 2 tablespoons butter and ¼ cup/1 oz/25 g plain (all-purpose) flour worked into a ball and stirred into the liquid, simmering for 5 minutes.

Nepalese Pork Curry (Songoor Ko Tarkari)

1½ lb/675 g blade (shoulder butt) of pork
3 tablespoons oil
2 large onions
4 garlic cloves
2 teaspoons ground cumin
6 dry red chillies
1 teaspoon ground cinnamon
3 teaspoons ground coriander
1 teaspoon salt
½ cup/¼ pint/375 ml water
½ cup/¼ pint/125 ml natural yogurt

Heat the oil in a large frying pan and fry the minced onion, crushed garlic, cumin, chillies, cinnamon, coriander and salt for 10 minutes, stirring continuously. Add the cubed pork and brown on all sides. Stir in the water and then the yogurt. Cover with a lid and cook gently for 2 hours. Serve with boiled rice.

Crusty Pork Casserole

1½ lb/675 g pork shoulder
½ lb/225 g large pork sausages
1 onion
3 carrots
3 celery sticks
1 tablespoon plain (all-purpose) flour
2 cups/1 pint/500 ml chicken stock
½ teaspoon rosemary
1 teaspoon soy sauce
Salt and pepper

Topping
8 × ½ in/1.25 cm French loaf slices
French mustard

Fry cubed pork and sausages together gently in their own fat until the sausages are lightly browned. Remove pork to a shallow casserole and add sausages, cut into 1-in/2.5-cm pieces. Fry chopped onion, sliced carrot and chopped celery together for 5 minutes in remaining pork fat. Stir in flour and blend in stock. Bring to the boil, stirring, and add remaining ingredients. Pour over meat, cover and cook at 350°F/180°C/Gas Mark 4 for 45 minutes. Spread bread liberally with mustard and place on the casserole, mustard side uppermost. Press bread down into casserole and return to the oven, uncovered, for 45 minutes.

Pork Chops with Cabbage

Illustrated on pages 124/125

4 pork chops
1½ lb/675 g cabbage
Salt and pepper
2 tablespoons butter
1 large onion
1 garlic clove
1 cup/½ pint/250 ml dry cider
4 tablespoons whipping cream
½ cup/2 oz/50 g Cheddar cheese

Finely shred the cabbage and cook in boiling salted water for 5 minutes. Drain and turn into a bowl. Melt 1 tablespoon butter in a frying pan, add the finely chopped onion and crushed garlic and fry gently for 10 minutes. Add the onion to the cabbage, mix lightly and turn half of it into the bottom of a casserole.

Heat the remainder of the butter in the frying pan, season the chops with salt and pepper and fry quickly on both sides until golden brown. Remove from the pan and place on the cabbage in the casserole. Cover with the remaining cabbage. Pour the cider into the pan and cook over a moderate heat until the cider has reduced to about 4 tablespoons.

Remove from the heat, stir in the cream and pour over the cabbage. Cover and bake at 350°F/180°C/Gas Mark 4 for 45 minutes. Remove from the oven, sprinkle grated cheese on top and bake uncovered for 30 minutes until the cheese is golden brown.

Tasmanian Pork Chops

4 thick loin pork chops
2 cups/4 oz/100 g sage and onion stuffing
1 eating apple
1 tablespoon honey
1 cup/½ pint/250 ml white wine

Cut the chops through the middle from the outer edge toward the bone, taking care the meat is still attached to the bone, and open out. Using a wooden rolling pin pound both sides to flatten. Peel and core apple and cut in 8 slices. Spread the stuffing on one side of chops and top with 2 apple slices. Spread other side with honey. Fold over and tie securely with string or tough thread. Put in the bottom of a shallow ovenproof dish and pour wine over. Cover and bake at 375°F/190°C/Gas Mark 5 for 1 hour. Remove lid for last 20 minutes' baking time so that chops brown. Untie chops and serve with liquid from dish.

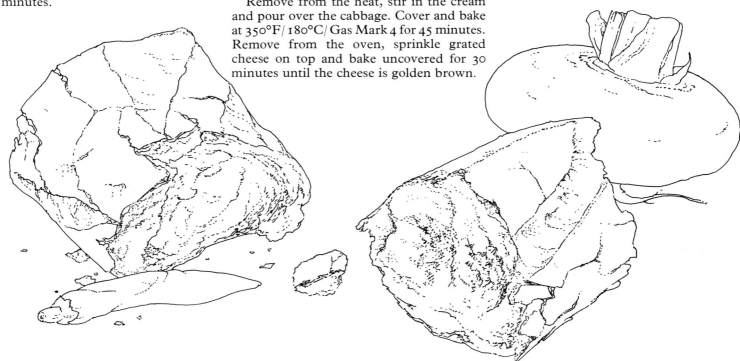

Bacon and Vegetable Risotto

8 slices of bacon (streaky)
1 cup/½ lb/225 g green peas
1 sweet red pepper
1 medium onion
½ lb/225 g fresh mushrooms
1¼ cups/8 oz/225 g short-grain rice
1 garlic clove
1 cup/4 oz/100 g grated Parmesan cheese
¼ cup/2 oz/50 g butter
3 cups/1½ pints/750 ml
beef or chicken stock
Salt and pepper to taste
½ teaspoon dried saffron

Cook the peas; remove the seeds from the red pepper, cook it briefly until *al dente* and slice it in large chunks; slice and grill (broil) the mushrooms; keep the peas, red pepper and mushrooms warm in the oven. Grill (broil) the bacon until crisp and keep warm in the oven.

Peel and chop the onion and garlic. Sauté both in 2 tablespoons/1 oz/25 g of butter in a heavy pan until golden. Add uncooked rice to the pan and cook briefly over moderate heat, stirring continuously until the rice has absorbed all of the butter. Add 1 cup/½ pint/250 ml of the boiling stock to the rice stirring continuously. Dissolve the saffron in some of the remaining stock. Stir the remaining stock into the rice mixture very slowly. It should take 15–20 minutes to add all the stock by which time the liquid should have been absorbed and the rice tender. Do not let the rice dry out. Season to taste with salt and pepper.

Pour remaining melted butter over the rice and add the cooked vegetables and bacon. Stir in the Parmesan cheese and serve immediately.

Porker's Hotpot

¾ lb/350 g pork belly (flank)
¾ lb/350 g pig's liver
2 tablespoons lard or dripping(s)
1 large onion
2 large carrots
3 celery sticks
¼ cup/1 oz/25 g plain (all-purpose) flour
1½ cups/¾ pint/375 ml chicken stock
¼ teaspoon sage
Salt and pepper

Savory Topping
2 cups/8 oz/225 g plain (all-purpose) flour
2 teaspoons baking powder
1 teaspoon onion or celery salt
Pepper
¼ cup/2 oz/50 g margarine or butter
5 tablespoons milk
A little extra milk for glazing
1 tablespoon medium oatmeal

Melt lard or dripping(s) in a large frying pan and fry sliced pork belly (flank) on both sides until golden. Remove and place in a 3 pint/1½ liter casserole. Quickly fry liver slices on each side for 2 minutes then add to the pork. Fry chopped vegetables gently in remaining fat for 10 minutes. Sprinkle over flour, stir in and cook for a further 3 minutes. Gradually stir in stock and bring to the boil, stirring all the time. Add sage and seasoning and pour over pork and liver. Stir gently, cover and cook in a moderate oven, 350°F/180°C/Gas Mark 4 for 1 hour.

Savory Topping: Sift together flour, baking powder and seasonings. Rub in the fat until mixture resembles fine breadcrumbs, then bind with milk to give a soft but not sticky dough. On a lightly floured surface roll dough out to a circle large enough to cover the top of the casserole. Mark into 4 wedge-shaped portions with a sharp knife. Remove casserole from oven and increase oven temperature to 400°F/200°C/Gas Mark 6. Taste and adjust seasoning, if necessary. Arrange the pastry round on top, brush over the top with milk and sprinkle with oatmeal. Replace in the oven for 30 minutes or until the topping is well risen and golden brown.

Pork Chops in Cider

4 pork chops
Salt and pepper
2 tablespoons oil
2 tablespoons butter
Sprig of parsley
Sprig of thyme
2 medium onions
½ cup/¼ pint/125 ml cider
½ cup/¼ pint/125 ml water

Trim excess fat from the chops and season well with salt and pepper. Heat the oil, add the butter and fry chops on both sides until brown. Put into an ovenproof dish with the herbs. Chop the onions finely and cook in the fat left in the pan until soft and golden. Add the onions to the chops, pour on the cider and water, cover and bake at 325°F/170°C/Gas Mark 3 for 1 hour.

Fruited Pork Chops

4 pork chops
¾ cup/4 oz/100 g raisins or sultanas
1 cup/4 oz/100 g dried apricots
Juice of 4 oranges
¼ teaspoon curry powder
1 teaspoon salt

Brown chops on both sides in a heavy pan. Add raisins or sultanas and chopped apricots. Combine juice of oranges with curry powder and salt and pour over chops. Cover and cook over very low heat for 1 hour, or bake at 350°F/180°C/Gas Mark 4 for 1 hour. Be sure there is enough juice, or add a little water to prevent chops from burning, but the finished dish should have only just enough sauce to coat the chops and fruit.

Spiced Pressed Pork

3 lb/1.5 kg pork belly (flank)
4 tablespoons vinegar
2 tablespoons oil
½ teaspoon salt
½ teaspoon ground nutmeg
½ teaspoon ground cinnamon
½ teaspoon ground ginger
¼ teaspoon black pepper

Bone the pork. With a sharp knife score pork rind in diamond shapes. Mix remaining ingredients. Put pork into shallow dish, pour marinade over and allow to stand for at least 3 hours, turning frequently. Wrap roast loosely in cooking foil and place in roasting pan. Cook at 350°F/180°C/Gas Mark 4 for 2 hours. Remove foil and place meat between two plates. Put heavy weight on top plate and leave until cold. Slice and serve cold.

Pork, Liver and Bacon Loaf

1 lb/450 g boned pork belly (flank)
½ lb/225 g pig's liver
8 slices of lean bacon
2 eggs
1 garlic clove
Pepper
1 tablespoon brandy

Mince the pork, liver and half the bacon coarsely. Line an ovenproof dish with the remaining slices of bacon. Beat the eggs lightly and add the crushed garlic, pepper and brandy. Stir into the minced (ground) meat and pack into the dish, pressing down firmly. Cover with foil and bake at 325°F/170°C/Gas Mark 3 for 2 hours. Serve hot, or leave until cold and turn out to serve with salad.

Pork and Bacon Loaf

Illustrated on pages 168/169

1 lb/450 g pork belly (flank)
½ lb/225 g unsmoked back bacon
2 cups/8 oz/225 g white breadcrumbs
1 onion
1 teaspoon dry mustard
½ teaspoon mixed herbs
Salt and pepper
1 egg
8 tablespoons cider

Mince (grind up or chop finely) the pork and bacon and chop the onion. Thoroughly mix pork, bacon and all dry ingredients in bowl. Add egg and cider to bind. Put on to a floured board and form into a rectangular shape. Put on a baking sheet or into a rectangular loaf dish and bake, uncovered, at 350°F/180°C/Gas Mark 4 for 1½ hours. Cool overnight and serve in slices.

Spanish Hot Meat Loaf

Illustrated on page 177

½ lb/225 g raw minced (ground) pork
½ lb/225 g raw minced (ground) beef
½ lb/225 g pork sausagemeat
4 slices white bread,
soaked in water, then squeezed dry
2 tablespoons chopped parsley
2 tablespoons tomato purée
1 teaspoon salt
Pepper
2 eggs
⅓ cup/2 oz/50 g Spanish stuffed green olives
1 lb/450 g can of ratatouille or peperonata

Mix pork, beef and sausagemeat in a bowl. Mash bread with a fork and add with parsley, purée, seasoning and eggs. Mix all together to blend smoothly. Distribute the sliced olives evenly over the bottom of a greased 2 lb/1 kg loaf pan. Cover with the ratatouille or peperonata, spreading it evenly. Put the meat mixture on top, level the top and cover with foil. Place loaf pan in a roasting pan with 1 in/2.5 cm of water in bottom and cook at 350°F/180°C/Gas Mark 4. Run a knife around the sides of the meat loaf, turn out on to a hot dish and serve sliced.

Devilled Pork Chops

Recipe on page 139

Pork chops
Prepared mustard
Brown sugar
Melted butter
Salt and pepper
Cashew nuts or peanuts

Somerset Pork with Cider Cream Sauce

Illustrated on page 120 (inset)

1 lb/450 g pork fillet (or 8 thin pork steaks)
¼ cup/1 oz/25 g plain (all-purpose) flour
¼ cup/2 oz/50 g butter
1 large onion
1⅓ cups/6 oz/175 g mushrooms
1 cup/½ pint/250 ml cider
Salt and pepper
4 tablespoons whipping cream
Chopped parsley

Cut pork fillet into 8 pieces. Place each piece between 2 sheets greaseproof (wax) paper, and beat with a meat hammer or a wooden rolling pin until ¼ in/0.75 cm thick. Coat pork with flour. Melt butter and fry pork slowly for about 3 minutes on each side. Drain well, and keep pork warm. Add onions and mushrooms to pan, and cook gently until tender but not brown. Stir in remaining flour, and cook for a minute. Remove from heat, and gradually stir in cider. Return to heat, stirring, and cook for a minute. Add cooked pork and seasoning, then stir in cream. Heat through, but do not boil. Serve garnished with chopped parsley.

Caraway Pork

½ lb/225 g lean pork
Seasoned flour
½ teaspoon caraway seeds
⅔ cup/2 oz/50 g button mushrooms
2 tablespoons dripping(s)
1 cup/½ pint/250 ml stock
2 tablespoons cream

Melt dripping(s), add sliced mushrooms and caraway seeds and cook for 2 minutes. Cut meat into strips, toss thoroughly in the seasoned flour and add to the pan. Cook quickly until sealed. Add the stock, bring to the boil and simmer, covered, for 20 minutes, or until pork is tender and cooked through. Stir in the cream and reheat but do not boil.

Pork Fillet en Croûte

1 lb/450 g pork fillet
Salt and pepper
4 cups/1 lb/450 g puff pastry
2 thin ham slices
1 egg

Stuffing
4 cups/1 lb/450 g mushrooms
1 large onion
¼ cup/2 oz/50 g butter
Salt and pepper
Pinch of thyme
2 tablespoons chopped parsley
4 tablespoons fresh breadcrumbs
2 eggs

Season the fillet well with salt and pepper and brown quickly on all sides. Cool. Roll out pastry to give a shape 2 in/5 cm longer than the fillet and about 10 in/25 cm wide. Put the fillet in the center of the pastry. Make up the stuffing. To do this, chop the mushrooms and onion finely and cook in the butter until the onion is just soft and golden. Season with salt and pepper, and add thyme, parsley and breadcrumbs. Stir in beaten eggs and mix well. Spread this mixture over the pork fillet and top with the ham slices. Form the pastry into a parcel and put folded ends down on the baking sheet. Brush with beaten egg, prick lightly with a fork and bake at 400°F/200°C/Gas Mark 6 for 45 minutes.

Pork and Bacon Escalopes

½ lb/225 g pork
8 slices of bacon
1 onion
1 garlic clove
Pinch of mixed herbs
Salt and pepper
1 egg
Melted lard

Mince the pork, bacon, onion and garlic finely. Add the herbs and sufficient egg to bind. Divide the mixture into 6 and put out into thin round medallions. Fry in hot lard for 3–5 minutes each side. Serve in sandwiches or in crusty rolls at a barbecue, or with mixed salad.

Topped Pork

1 lb/450 g pork shoulder
A little seasoned flour
1 lb/450 g root vegetables
1 cup/½ pint/250 ml stock or cider
Salt and pepper
½ teaspoon mixed herbs
2 cups/8 oz/225 g
self-raising (self-rising) flour
Salt
⅓ cup/3 oz/75 g butter or margarine
1 egg
A little milk

Toss the pork in the seasoned flour and mix with the vegetables. Put into a pie pan and add the stock or cider, salt, pepper and herbs. Cover with foil and cook at 325°F/170°C/Gas Mark 3 for about 1¼ hours. Sift the flour and salt into a bowl and rub in the butter. Mix to a stiff dough with the egg and milk (save a little for brushing on top). Roll out a little larger than the dish and cut into 2-in/5-cm squares. Brush over with egg and arrange, overlapping on top of the hot meat and vegetables. Cook at 425°F/220°C/Gas Mark 6 for 15 minutes.

Citrus Pork

4 pork chops
¼ cup/2 oz/50 g butter
3 tablespoons oil
2 onions
6 slices back bacon
1 cup/½ pint/250 ml dry white wine
2 teaspoons tomato purée
1 cup/½ pint/250 ml chicken stock
1¼ cups/4 oz/100 g mushrooms
Sprig of parsley
Sprig of thyme
1 bay leaf
Salt and pepper
1 lemon
1 orange

Heat butter and oil together and fry chops on both sides about 20 minutes. Remove from the pan and keep warm. Fry chopped onions and chopped bacon without browning. Stir in the wine, tomato purée, stock and sliced mushrooms. Add herbs and cook uncovered for about 10 minutes until slightly reduced. Return chops to pan and heat through. Stir in orange and lemon rinds and the seasoning. Remove herbs. Garnish with chopped parsley and lemon and orange slices.

Porkburgers

1 lb/450 g pork shoulder
1 tablespoon chopped parsley
1 large onion
1 garlic clove
Flour
Salt and pepper
1 egg
Breadcrumbs

Mince (grind) the pork, parsley, onion and garlic twice. Season and form into 8 flat cakes. Dip in flour, beaten egg and breadcrumbs. Fry for 5 minutes on each side.

Sparerib Chops with Almonds

4 sparerib chops
1 tablespoon prepared mustard
1 tablespoon brown sugar
¼ cup/1 oz/25 g shredded almonds
Salt and pepper

Mix the mustard and sugar together and rub over the chops. Grill (broil) until tender. Sprinkle almonds over the pork and season with salt and pepper. Return under grill (broiler) to brown the almonds.

Pork and Apple Casserole

Recipe on page 142

Boned blade or shoulder of pork
Flour
Dry mustard
Salt and pepper
Butter
Cooking oil
Onions
Dried sage
Dried thyme
Dry white wine
Apples

138

Pork Pudding

¾ lb/350g diced pork belly (flank)
1½ cups/6 oz/175 g
self-raising (self-rising) flour
1 cup/4 oz/100 g shredded suet
Salt and pepper
A little milk
1 large onion or leek
1 large potato
1 teaspoon sage
Stock or beer

Make the pastry by mixing the flour, suet and seasonings together to a soft dough with the milk. Put the pork, chopped onion and potato in a 4-cup/2-pint/1-liter pudding basin (steaming mold), add the sage and season well. Moisten with stock or beer. Roll out pastry, shape it to fit the basin (mold), then cover with pastry. Cover with a piece of greased foil and steam for 2 hours. Serve with rich gravy.

Tropical Pork Salad

¾ lb/350g cooked pork
1 apple
2 celery sticks
1 grapefruit
⅔ cup/2 oz/50 g walnuts
½ cup/¼ pint/125 ml sour cream
Salt and pepper
4 large lettuce leaves
Pinch of ground ginger

Chop the pork, apple and celery. Divide grapefruit into segments and chop. Chop the walnuts. Combine first seven ingredients together. Divide mixture between lettuce leaves and sprinkle with ginger.

Pork and Pâté Parcels

6 pork chops
3 cups/12 oz/350 g puff pastry
¼ lb/100 g pork liver pâté
Salt and pepper
1 egg

Clean ends of bones and grill (broil) chops for 5 minutes each side. Leave to cool. Roll out pastry to 18 × 12 in/45 × 30 cm and divide into 6-in/15-cm squares. Spread chops on both sides with pâté and season. Wrap chops in pastry, leaving bones protruding. Seal edges. Brush with beaten egg. Bake at 375°F/190°C/Gas Mark 5 for 30 minutes.

Italian Pork and Ham Slices

4 slices unsmoked ham (gammon)
4 thin pork steaks
4 slices Gruyère cheese

Grill (broil) ham slices on one side. Turn, and place pork steaks alongside. Grill (broil) both. Put one slice of cheese on each slice of ham. Cover with pork steaks, grilled (broiled) side down. Put back under grill (broiler) to cook remaining sides of pork. Serve on a bed of cooked pasta with hot tomato or mushroom sauce.

Sweet and Sour Pork

8 thick slices pork belly (flank)
¼ lb/100 g cooked noodles

Sauce
1 tablespoon cornstarch
½ cup/¼ pint/125 ml cider
2 tablespoons brown sugar
1 tablespoon red currant jelly
1 tablespoon soy sauce
2 tablespoons vinegar

Grill (broil) pork slices 10 minutes each side. Meanwhile make sauce by blending cornstarch with a little cider. Put into pan with remaining cider, sugar, jelly and soy sauce. Bring to boil, stirring, and then simmer for 5 minutes. Add vinegar. Serve pork on a bed of noodles with sauce poured over.

Devilled Pork Chops

Illustrated on pages 132/133

4 large (or 8 small) pork chops
1 tablespoon prepared mustard
1 tablespoon brown sugar
1 tablespoon melted butter
Salt and pepper
$\frac{1}{3}$ cup/2 oz/50 g cashew nuts or peanuts

Mix the mustard, brown sugar, melted butter, salt and pepper and spread half the mixture over the chops. Grill (broil) for 7 minutes. Turn over the chops and spread with remaining mixture. Grill (broil) for 7 minutes. Sprinkle on the coarsely chopped nuts and return to grill (broiler) until the nuts are golden brown.

Honey Glazed Pork Fillet

Illustrated on page 141

2 pork fillets (tenderloins)
3 slices of lean bacon
12 large soaked prunes
12 whole almonds
Salt and pepper
3 tablespoons clear honey
$\frac{1}{2}$ cup/$\frac{1}{4}$ pint/125 ml cider

Soak the prunes overnight in water. Dip the almonds in boiling water, then in cold water, and rub off their skins. Remove any fat from the fillets and take away the silvery thread which runs half way along the fillets. With a sharp knife make a slit down the length of both pork fillets and open them out gently. Stone the prunes and fill each with an almond. Place the stuffed prunes along the center of one fillet, season with salt and pepper and place the second fillet on top. Tie the fillets together firmly with string and place in a roasting pan. Cut the slices of bacon into strips lengthways. Wrap these strips around the fillets. Spoon 2 tablespoons honey over the top and pour over the cider. Roast at 375°F/190°C/Gas Mark 5 for 1 hour, basting occasionally with the pan juices. About 10 minutes before the end of cooking time, add the remaining honey to ensure a shiny glaze. Serve with rice.

Hand Raised Pork Pie

Filling
1$\frac{1}{4}$ lb/550 g pork shoulder
$\frac{1}{2}$ teaspoon sage
Salt and pepper

Pastry
3 cups/12 oz/350 g
self-raising (self-rising) flour
$\frac{1}{2}$ teaspoon salt
$\frac{1}{2}$ cup/4 oz/100 g lard
$\frac{1}{2}$ cup/$\frac{1}{4}$ pint/125 ml water
1 egg

Jelly
Pork bones or a trotter (foot)
4 cups/2 pints/1 liter water
1 onion
Salt and pepper
1 teaspoon gelatine

Sift the flour and salt into a bowl. Boil the lard and water in a pan and then pour into center of the flour. Work all together into a smooth dough. Gradually mold two-thirds to form a bowl shape (a cake dish can be used as a guide). Put on a greased baking sheet and fill the center with mixture of the diced pork, sage and seasoning. Roll out the reserved third as a lid, brush edges of the pie with beaten egg and seal the lid on. Use trimmings to form leaves for decoration. Make a hole in the top and brush over pie with egg. Bake in oven at 409°F/200°C/Gas Mark 6 for 30 minutes, then reduce heat to 350°F/180°C/Gas Mark 4 for a further 1$\frac{1}{2}$ hours. Make a jelly from the bones or trotter, water, onion and seasoning by boiling for 2 hours. Strain, and add the dissolved gelatine. Allow to cool. Pour some of this into the hole in the pie lid when cool and leave to set before cutting.

Honeyed Pork Chops

Recipe on page 142

Pork loin chops
Soy sauce
Garlic
Clear honey

Honey Glazed Pork Fillet

Recipe on page 139

Pork fillets/tenderloin
Lean bacon
Prunes
Almonds
Salt and pepper
Clear honey
Cider

142

Pork Salad with Yogurt Dressing

1 lb/450g cooked pork
½ cucumber
1 green pepper
4 large lettuce leaves
2 tomatoes

Dressing
½ cup/¼ pint/125ml natural yogurt
1 tablespoon chopped chives
¼ teaspoon dry mustard
¼ teaspoon garlic salt
1 teaspoon wine vinegar or lemon juice
Salt and pepper

Mix diced pork, cucumber and green pepper together in a bowl. Prepare the dressing by mixing all the ingredients thoroughly. Pour dressing over pork and toss lightly. Serve on lettuce leaves with sliced tomatoes.

Pork and Apple Casserole

Illustrated on pages 136/137

2 lb/1kg boned blade or shoulder of pork
5 tablespoons plain (all-purpose) flour
2 teaspoons dry mustard
Salt and pepper
¼ cup/2oz/50g butter
2 tablespoons cooking oil
2 medium onions
1 teaspoon dried sage
1 teaspoon dried thyme
1 cup/½ pint/250ml dry white wine
1 lb/450g apples

Put the flour and dry mustard in a bowl and season with salt and pepper. Cut the pork into cubes and toss in the seasoned flour. Heat the butter and oil in a pan and fry the sliced onions until soft and golden. Add the pork and fry until golden brown. Stir in any excess flour, and add the herbs, stock and wine. Bring to the boil, reduce heat, cover the pan and simmer gently for 1½ hours. Core the apples and slice them thickly. Add to the pan and continue cooking for 30 minutes. If preferred, the casserole may be cooked in the oven at 350°F/180°C/Gas Mark 4.

Honeyed Pork Chops

Illustrated on page 140

4 pork loin chops
2 tablespoons soy sauce
1 tablespoon clear honey
1 garlic clove

Trim any surplus fat from the chops. Blend together the soy sauce, honey and crushed garlic and pour into a shallow dish. Turn the prepared chops in the liquid and cover the dish. Leave for several hours or overnight in the refrigerator or other cold place. Drain the chops and put into a shallow ovenproof dish. Spoon on the liquid and cover with a lid or foil. Bake at 375°F/190°C/Gas Mark 5 for 40 minutes. Remove the cover and continue cooking for 20 minutes. Serve garnished with parsley and accompanied by rice.

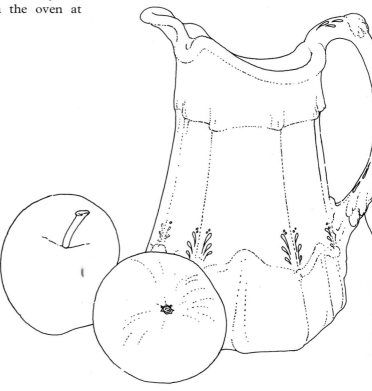

Cider Sausage Hotpot

Illustrated on page 104

1 lb / 450 g pork sausages
1 small red cabbage
1 onion
2 red-skinned apples
2 teaspoons juniper berries
1 cup / ½ pint / 250 ml cider
3 tablespoons red currant jelly
1 tablespoon vinegar
Salt and pepper

Spiced orange slices
2 oranges
½ cup / ¼ pint / 125 ml water
¼ cup / 2 oz / 50 g sugar
Pinch of ground cinnamon

Put the sausages into a casserole with the shredded cabbage, chopped onion, sliced apple and juniper berries. Add the cider, red currant jelly, vinegar, salt and pepper. Cover and cook at 300°F / 150°C / Gas Mark 2 for 3 hours. Serve with spiced orange slices, made by simmering sliced oranges in water and sugar flavored with cinnamon until glazed and tender.

Sausage and Mushroom Pie

Illustrated on page 144

1 lb / 450 g sausages
2 medium onions
2 oz / 50 g butter
¼ cup / 5 tablespoons
plain (all-purpose) flour
1 cup / ½ pint / 250 ml milk
½ cup / ¼ pint / 125 ml stock
Salt and pepper
1 cup / 4 oz / 100 g button mushrooms
3 cups / 12 oz / 350 g puff pastry
Beaten egg to glaze

Grill (broil) the sausages until cooked. Slice the onion and fry in the butter until soft and golden. Stir in the flour and cook for 1 minute. Gradually add the milk and stock and bring to the boil. Simmer until thick and then season with salt and pepper. Stir in the mushrooms. Put the sausages into a pie dish and spoon the sauce and mushrooms over the top. Cover the pie with pastry and use trimmings for decoration. Brush with beaten egg. Bake at 400°F / 200°C / Gas Mark 6 for 40 minutes. If desired, cooked peas, corn, red or green peppers may be used instead of mushrooms.

Sausage Toad-in-the-Hole

1 lb / 450 g pork sausagemeat
1 cup / 4 oz / 100 g plain (all-purpose) flour
Pinch of salt
1 egg
1 cup / ½ pint / 250 ml milk

Divide the sausagemeat into 8 portions and roll each portion into a sausage shape. Put into a roasting pan. Bake at 400°F / 200°C / Gas Mark 6 for 10 minutes. To make the batter, sift the flour and salt into a bowl. Add the egg and half the milk and beat until smooth. Add the remaining milk and beat well. Pour the batter over the sausages and cook for a further 20–30 minutes until the batter is well risen and golden brown and the sausages cooked.

Sausage and Apple Loaf

1½ lb / 675 g pork sausagemeat
¾ lb / 350 g cooking apples
1 large onion
1 cup / 2 oz / 50 g fresh white breadcrumbs
2 tablespoons Worcestershire sauce
6 slices cooked ham

Peel the apples and grate them. Mix thoroughly all ingredients, except the ham slices. Line bottom and sides of a 2-lb / 1-kg loaf pan with ham slices. Do not trim slices if they are too big. Fill pan with the meat mixture and fold over ham slices, if necessary. Cover with cooking foil and place pan in a larger pan, filled about one-third full with hot water. Bake at 375°F / 190°C / Gas Mark 5 for 1½ hours. Cool in pan completely before turning out to serve with salad.

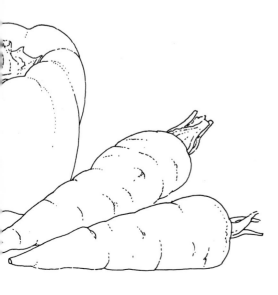

Sausage and Mushroom Pie

Recipe on page 143

Sausages
Onions
Butter
Flour
Milk
Stock
Salt and pepper
Button mushrooms
Puff pastry
Egg

Sausage and Chicken Liver Terrine

Recipe on page 146

Pork sausages
Chicken livers
Garlic
Salt and pepper
Mixed herbs
Onion
Bacon
Eggs
Sherry
Olives
Red pimento
Aspic jelly

Sausage and Chicken Liver Terrine

Illustrated on page 145

1 lb/450 g pork sausages
½ lb/225 g chicken livers
1 garlic clove
Salt and pepper
1 teaspoon mixed herbs
1 medium onion
6 slices of bacon
2 eggs
2 tablespoons sherry
10 stuffed olives
1 canned red pimento
Aspic jelly

Skin the sausages. Mix with chopped chicken livers, crushed garlic, salt, pepper, herbs, finely chopped onion and 4 finely chopped strips of bacon. Mix with eggs and sherry. Put half the mixture into an earthenware terrine. Halve the olives and cut the pimento into strips. Arrange over the bottom layer of the terrine. Top with the remaining mixture and press down well. Put the remaining strips of bacon on top. Cover with a piece of greased wax paper and a lid. Stand the terrine in a roasting pan of hot water and cook at 325°F/170°C/Gas Mark 3 for 1½ hours. Cool under weights. When completely cold, glaze with liquid aspic which may be lightly colored if liked. Serve with hot toast.

Sausage Braid

1 lb/450 g pork sausagemeat
3 cups/12 oz/350 g pastry
3 teaspoons French mustard
1 small onion
½ teaspoon mixed herbs
2 hard-boiled eggs
1 egg

Roll out pastry to a 12-in/30-cm square. Spread mustard on pastry. Mix together sausagemeat, chopped onion and mixed herbs, and place half of this mixture down center third of the pastry, leaving ½ in/1.25 cm at top and bottom. Arrange hard-boiled eggs on top of sausagemeat, then cover with remaining sausagemeat. Cut in from the edges to within ½ in/1.25 cm of the filling at 1-in/2.5-cm intervals on both sides of the filling. Brush edges of pastry with beaten egg. Fold in the ½ in/1.25 cm of pastry at top and bottom and fold alternate strips of pastry from the sides over the filling to form a braid, and to cover filling. Place on a baking sheet and brush braid with beaten egg. Bake at 400°F/200°C/Gas Mark 6 for 20 minutes, then reduce to 350°F/180°C/Gas Mark 4 and continue cooking for a further 15 minutes. Serve hot or cold.

Sausage, Mushroom and Kidney Roll

Illustrated on pages 148/149

4 pork sausages
1¾ cups/6 oz/150 g kidney
1 onion
3 tablespoons oil
1 cup/3 oz/75 g mushrooms
Salt and pepper
3 cups/12 oz/350 g pastry
½ cup/2 oz/50 g grated cheese
Beaten egg to glaze

Chop the onion, kidney and mushrooms. Cook the sausages and chop them. Fry the onion in the oil until soft and golden. Add the kidney and mushrooms and fry gently for 3 minutes. Mix with the sausage pieces and seasoning to taste. Roll pastry to an oblong 12 × 10 in (30 × 15 cm). Brush edges with beaten egg and sprinkle with grated cheese. Spread the sausage mixture evenly on top of the pastry and roll up like a carpet, making sure the filling is securely enclosed. Put on to a baking sheet and brush with beaten egg. Decorate with shapes cut from pastry trimmings. Bake at 375°F/190°C/Gas Mark 5 for 45 minutes until golden brown, and serve hot or cold.

Sausage and Potato Loaf

Illustrated on page 105

1 cup/8 oz/225 g mashed potato
1 cup/4 oz/100 g sage and onion stuffing
Salt and pepper
½ lb/225 g pork sausages
3 hard-boiled eggs
1 large tomato
¼ cup/1 oz/25 g grated cheese

Combine the mashed potato and stuffing, and season well. Grease and line a loaf pan with greased wax paper. Put in half the potato mixture. Arrange the sausages in two rows on top with the hard-boiled eggs running down the center. Top with the remaining potato mixture. Cover with another piece of greased wax paper and bake at 375°F/190°C/Gas Mark 5 for 1¼ hours. Cool for 5 minutes and unmold on to an ovenproof dish. Top with sliced tomato and sprinkle with cheese. Bake for 20 minutes. Serve hot or cold.

Sausage and Cabbage Hotpot

1 lb/450 g sausages
2 medium onions
2 tablespoons butter
3 medium carrots
½ small cabbage
2 tablespoons tomato purée
1 cup/½ pint/250 ml ale or beef stock
½ cup/¼ pint/125 ml water
Salt and pepper

Cut the sausages in half and fry with sliced onions in butter until lightly browned. Put into a casserole with thinly sliced carrots and coarsely shredded cabbage. Mix tomato purée with ale or stock and water and pour into casserole. Season well, cover and cook at 400°F/200°C/Gas Mark 6 for 1 hour.

Sausage and Cabbage Provençal

1 lb/450 g sausages
6 strips of bacon (streaky)
1 green cabbage
2 medium onions
½ lb/225 g tomatoes
½ cup/¼ pint/125 ml red wine
1 cup/½ pint/250 ml stock
Salt and pepper
1 tablespoon concentrated tomato paste
1 garlic clove
1 tablespoon brown sugar

Shred the cabbage and slice the onions and tomatoes. Chop the bacon. Arrange vegetables, sausages and bacon in layers in a casserole. Mix the wine, stock, salt, pepper, tomato paste, crushed garlic and sugar and pour into the casserole. Cover and cook at 325°F/170°C/Gas Mark 3 for 1½ hours. Serve topped with cubes of toasted bread.

Sausage and Vegetable Brunch

Illustrated on pages 184/185

4 cooked sausages
1 medium onion
1 red pepper
3 tablespoons oil
1 garlic clove
4 tablespoons cooked peas
4 eggs

Slice the onion and pepper and fry gently in oil for 5 minutes. Add the crushed garlic and sliced sausages, and season to taste with salt and pepper. Cook for 3 minutes and stir in the peas. Divide between four individual ovenproof dishes and make a hollow in the center of each. Crack an egg into each hollow. Stand the dishes on a baking sheet. Bake at 375°F/190°C/Gas Mark 5 for 15 minutes until the egg whites are set but the yolks still soft.

Pork Sausages in Red Wine

1 lb/450 g pork sausages
¾ lb/350 g new potatoes
2 onions
2 tablespoons oil
¼ cup/1 oz/25 g plain (all-purpose) flour
¼ cup/½ pint/250 ml beef stock
¼ cup/½ pint/250 ml red wine
Salt and pepper

Put the sausages in a casserole with the scraped potatoes. If only old potatoes are available, peel and cube them. Slice the onions and cook in the oil for 3 minutes. Stir in the flour and cook for 1 minute. Add the stock, wine and seasoning and bring to the boil. Pour over the sausages and potatoes. Cover and cook at 350°F/180°C/Gas Mark 4 for 1¼ hours. Skim off fat from the surface before serving.

Sausage, Mushroom and Kidney Roll

Recipe on page 146

Pork sausages
Kidney
Onion
Oil
Mushrooms
Salt and pepper
Pastry
Grated cheese
Egg

Skewered Sausage Meatballs

Illustrated on pages 100/101

1 lb/450 g pork sausages
4 heaped tablespoons
sage and onion stuffing mix
Salt and pepper
8 button mushrooms
1 large red pepper
Bay leaves
4 tablespoons oil
2 tablespoons beer

Sauce
14 oz/400 g can of tomatoes
1 tablespoon concentrated tomato paste
1 tablespoon Worcestershire sauce
2 teaspoons French mustard

Skin the sausages and mix with the dry sage and onion stuffing mix. Season with salt and pepper. Form into 12 even-sized balls. Thread on to 4 kebab skewers with mushrooms, pepper cut into chunks and a few bay leaves. Mix the oil with the beer and brush each kebab. Grill (broil) on one side until crisp and golden. Turn the skewers, brush again with oil and beer and cook until crisp and golden. Simmer the sauce ingredients together for 5 minutes. Serve kebabs on cooked rice and cover with the sauce.

Bacon/Ham Kebabs

Illustrated on page 152

1½ lb/675 g thick ham (bacon) slices
2 tablespoons Worcestershire sauce
2 teaspoons prepared mustard
Juice of 1 lemon
1 tablespoon concentrated tomato paste
Salt and pepper
2 tablespoons oil
1 green pepper
1 medium onion
2 pineapple slices (fresh or canned)

Use two thick slices from a collar or smoked shoulder. If the meat is very salty soak it for 4 hours in cold water. Remove the slices, drain well, and cut into neat cubes. Put into a pan with fresh water and simmer for 20 minutes. Drain the ham cubes. Mix the sauce, mustard, lemon juice, tomato paste, salt, pepper and oil. Pour the mixture over the cubes while they are still warm. Leave to stand for 30 minutes. Remove the cubes from the liquid and thread on to two large or four small kebab skewers, alternating with chunks of pepper, onion and pineapple. Brush kebabs with some of the liquid and grill (broil) for 5 minutes. Turn the kebabs, brush with more liquid and grill (broil) for 6 minutes. Serve hot on a bed of rice.

Spiced Bacon/ Ham

Illustrated on pages 156/157

4 lb/2 kg solid piece of ham (or bacon)
2 cups/1 pint/500 ml cider
2 cups/1 pint/500 ml stock
⅔ cup/4 oz/100 g soaked prunes
4 cardamoms
4 cloves
Piece of root ginger
1 bay leaf
1 teaspoon peppercorns

Dumplings
½ cup/2 oz/50 g oatmeal
1 cup/4 oz/100 g
self-raising (self-rising) flour
⅓ cup/2 oz/50 g shredded suet
1 egg

Soak the meat overnight if necessary. Soak the prunes in cold water until plump. Put the meat into a large pan and add the cider, stock, prunes, crushed cardamoms, cloves, bruised ginger, bay leaf and crushed peppercorns. Bring to the boil and simmer for 1 hour 20 minutes. Make the dumplings by mixing the oatmeal, flour and suet and adding enough beaten egg to bind to a soft dough. Divide into small balls the size of a walnut. Add to the piece of meat and cover, and continue simmering for 20 minutes.

NOTE

In Europe there is a type of pig especially reared to produce certain proportions of lean meat to fat. The roasts and cuts of meat coming from this pig are called **Bacon** or **Gammon** joints and are generally **not available in countries outside Europe**. In these countries **cooked or uncooked, smoked** or **unsmoked ham or picnic shoulder may be substituted** where indicated in these recipes.

Molasses Glazed Ham/Bacon

5 lb/2½ kg bacon or ham
4 tablespoons molasses
12 peppercorns
1 bay leaf
½ cup/¼ pint/125 ml dry cider
Cloves for garnish

(Soak the meat overnight if too salty, and rinse.) Place the meat in a saucepan and cover with cold water. Add 2 tablespoons of the molasses, the peppercorns and the bay leaf; bring slowly to the boil and simmer for 1 hour (water must never come back to the boil). Drain the roast, strip off the skin and score the fat into diamonds with a sharp knife. Warm the remaining 2 tablespoons of molasses and pour over the fat surface. Place the ham in a roasting pan and pour the cider over the top. Cook in a moderate oven, 350°F/180°C/Gas Mark 4, for 1 hour, basting frequently with the cider. Decorate with cloves and serve hot or cold.

Bacon/Ham en Croûte

Illustrated on page 153

3 lb/1.5 kg
foreshank of ham (forehock of bacon)
½ lb/225 g stuffing mix
1 egg
1 onion
6 cups/1½ lb/675 g puff pastry
Beaten egg to glaze

If the meat is very salty, soak it overnight. Put the meat into a pan and cover with fresh water. Bring to the boil, reduce heat and simmer for 1½ hours. Drain and cool for 1 hour. The stuffing may be any flavoring, but chestnut is particularly delicious. Make up the stuffing with slightly less liquid than called for in the instructions. Add the egg and finely chopped onion. Spread over the top and sides of the meat to coat evenly. Roll out the puff pastry and cut one long side strip sufficiently large to wrap round the meat. Cut two circles to fit each end of the wrapped ham. Brush the pastry edges with beaten egg and pinch together to seal. Put on to a baking sheet and glaze with beaten egg. Decorate with shapes cut from pastry trimmings, and glaze with egg. Bake at 400°F/200°C/Gas Mark 6 for 45 minutes. Serve hot or cold, cut into slices.

Bacon/Ham with Cranberry Sauce Glaze

Illustrated on page 161

5 lb/2.5 kg boned bacon or ham
3½ cups/1¾ pints/1 liter cider
Water
¾ cup/6 oz/175 g
sugar (preferably demerara)
2 tablespoons cranberry sauce

(Soak meat overnight in water if necessary.) Place meat in a large saucepan. Pour in the cider and enough water to cover the meat. Boil, cover and simmer for 2 hours. Drain meat, but reserve liquid. Remove the skin, score lattice pattern over the fat, and place the meat in a roasting pan. Measure 1 cup/½ pint/250 ml cooking liquid into a pan (the rest can be made into flavorsome soups) with the sugar. Dissolve over a low heat, then boil for 5 minutes. Stir in cranberry sauce. Pour this over the meat. Bake at 400°F/200°C/Gas Mark 6 for 25 minutes, basting at least twice.

Bacon/Ham Kebabs

Recipe on page 150

Thick ham/bacon slices
Worcestershire sauce
Prepared mustard
Tomato paste
Salt and pepper
Oil
Green pepper
Onion
Pineapple slices

Bacon/Ham
en Croûte

Recipe on page 151

Foreshank of ham or forehock of bacon
Stuffing mix
Egg
Onion
Puff pastry

Roast Bacon/ Ham

2 lb/1 kg bacon or ham
1 lb/450 g potatoes
1 lb/450 g carrots
¼ cup/2 oz/50 g lard
Salt and pepper
2 tablespoons butter
Apple sauce

Wash the meat and wrap it in a single piece of foil. Peel and cut potatoes for roasting, scrape and slice carrots thinly. Heat oven to 425°F/220°C/Gas Mark 7. Melt the lard in a small roasting pan, add the potatoes and place the pan at the top of the oven. Put the roast in a separate roasting pan with 1 in/ 2.5 cm water and place it in the center of the oven. Put the carrots in an ovenproof dish with a little water, salt, pepper and butter. Cover and place them in the oven. Cook the meat and vegetables for 1½ hours, opening the foil round the meat for the final 30 minutes to brown the fat. Serve with apple sauce.

NOTE

In Europe there is a type of pig especially reared to produce certain proportions of lean meat to fat. The roasts and cuts of meat coming from this pig are called **Bacon** or **Gammon** joints and are generally **not available in countries outside Europe.** In these countries **cooked or uncooked, smoked or unsmoked ham or picnic shoulder may be substituted** where indicated in these recipes.

Stuffed Roast Bacon/Ham

3 lb/1.5 kg bacon or ham
¼ cup/2 oz/50 g butter
2 cups/4 oz/100 g fresh breadcrumbs
2 tablespoons chopped parsley
Grated rind of 1 lemon
2 teaspoons thyme
A little beaten egg
Pepper

Put the meat into a pan of cold water and bring to the boil. Discard the water. (This step may be omitted if the meat is not too salty.) Cover with fresh cold water, bring to the boil and simmer for 20 minutes. Melt the butter and stir in the breadcrumbs, parsley, lemon rind, thyme and enough egg to bind. Season with pepper. Drain the meat and strip off the rind. Insert the stuffing into the center of the meat and roll into a round, tied with string. Score fat in a criss-cross design and bake at 350°F/180°C/Gas Mark 4 for 1 hour. Tomatoes and potatoes can be baked in the oven at the same time to accompany the meal.

Bacon/Ham Parcels

4 lean bacon chops
(back bacon cut short and ½ in thick)
or uncooked ham steaks
Pepper
1 large onion
1 large apple
1 cup/4 oz/100 g mushrooms
4 slices Gruyère cheese

Cut four squares of foil 12 × 12 in/30 × 30 cm, and grease them with butter. Place a chop in the center of each piece of foil and season with pepper. Cover each chop with layers of (a) sliced onion, (b) sliced mushrooms, (c) sliced apple and (d) a slice of cheese. Fold up the ends of each parcel, place on a baking sheet and bake at 375°F/ 190°C/Gas Mark 5 for 45 minutes. Serve in the foil parcels.

Honey Roast Ham

Illustrated on page 160

5 lb/2.5 kg boned, rolled, unsmoked ham
2 tablespoons thick honey
1 cup/8 fl oz/200 ml orange juice
1 large orange
Arrowroot

(Soak the meat in cold water if too salty.) Cut the skin with a sharp knife into diamond shapes. Put into a roasting pan. Mix the honey and orange juice together and pour over the roast. Bake at 350°F/180°C/Gas Mark 4, basting frequently, for 20 minutes per lb/450 g and 20 minutes over. Strain off the liquid and add the grated rind of the orange and its chopped flesh. Thicken with a little arrowroot and serve in a gravy boat with the hot roast.

Green Ham

3 lb/1.5 kg gammon or ham
2 lb/1 kg knuckle of veal (flesh and bone)
1 calf's foot
1 onion
1 carrot
Sprig of thyme
Sprig of parsley
1 bottle dry white wine
1 teaspoon tarragon vinegar
4 tablespoons chopped parsley
4 white peppercorns
Salt

Scrub gammon (ham) and leave it to soak for several hours, then cover with fresh water, bring to boil slowly and let it simmer for 50 minutes. Meanwhile cover the cut up knuckle and split calf's foot with the wine, add onion, carrot, peppercorns, salt and herbs, and simmer in closed pan for the same time. Remove the meat from its water, wash it, peel off the rind and cut it into matchstick-sized lumps. Strain the wine stock. Pour the stock over the gammon and the calf's foot, cover and leave to simmer slowly until the ham is so soft it can be cut with a spoon. Strain the stock again in the same way as before and leave to cool so that the fat can be skimmed from the surface. Remove calf's foot, then crush the ham into pieces. Complete this breaking-up process with two forks, one in each hand. Melt the fat-free stock, add vinegar, adjust seasoning if necessary, stir in chopped parsley and pour it over the ham. Leave in a cold place to set.

Baked Ham Steaks with Apple

4 ham or gammon steaks
2 tablespoons butter
1 large onion
1 large cooking apple
1 cup/¼ pint/125 ml apple juice
2 tablespoons raisins or sultanas
Pepper
Chopped parsley

Heat oven to 400°F/200°C/Gas Mark 6. Remove rind (if any) and place the ham steaks in an ovenproof dish. Cook chopped onion in the butter until soft. Arrange over the steaks with the peeled and thinly sliced apple and the raisins or sultanas. Pour the apple juice over the steaks. Season with pepper. Cover with foil and cook in the center of the oven for 40 minutes. Remove and sprinkle with chopped parsley.

Bacon/Ham in a Jacket

3 lb/1.5 kg unsmoked bacon
(unsmoked ham roast)
2½ cups/10 oz/300 g
self-raising (self-rising) flour
½ cup/2 oz/50 g fine oatmeal
1 teaspoon salt
½ cup/4 oz/100 g lard
½ cup/¼ pint/125 ml water
1 egg yolk

Soak the meat for 2 hours in cold water to remove excess salt, and drain well. Strip off rind. Mix flour, oatmeal and salt. Melt the lard in the water over low heat and stir into the flour, kneading well. Roll out on a floured board and wrap the meat in a parcel of pastry. Brush over with the egg yolk and bake at 350°F/180°C/Gas Mark 4 for 1½ hours. This is very good served with hot tomato sauce or barbecue sauce.

Bacon Chops or Fresh Ham Steaks

Bacon chops come from the rib back area of a bacon side after the rib bones have been removed, and they usually weigh between 4–6 oz/100–175 g. They are tender and full of flavor, just like back bacon, which in fact is what they really are, only cut in slices ½ in/1.25 cm thick instead of being cut thinly. Outside Europe slices of fresh uncooked ham may be substituted.

The best way to cook them is to fry or grill (broil) for 5 minutes on each side at a medium heat. Tomatoes, mushrooms or eggs can be popped into the pan to cook alongside for the last few minutes. Bacon chops cook through very quickly so any potatoes to be served with them should be put to boil before the meat goes in the pan.

Fried Bacon or Ham Chops

Remove rind (if any) from the chops and snip the fat at intervals. Fry the meat gently in its own fat or add a little butter allowing 5 minutes for each side. Arrange the cooked chops on a dish and garnish with fried mushrooms and tomato.

Crumbed Bacon or Ham Chops

Remove rind (if any) and snip the fat at intervals. Dip chops in beaten egg and crumbs. Fry the breaded chops gently in butter for 10 minutes turning once. Use ½ cup/2 oz/50 g breadcrumbs and 1 beaten egg to coat 4 chops. Serve with peas and potatoes.

Sweet and Sour Chops

Heat together 3 tablespoons tomato ketchup, 1 teaspoon vinegar and 1 tablespoon brown sugar. Brush this mixture over 4 bacon or ham chops and cook them under a moderate grill (broiler) for 5 minutes. Turn chops, brush again with the tomato mixture and cook for 5 minutes.

Spiced Bacon/Ham

Recipe on page 150

Solid piece of bacon or ham
Cider
Stock
Prunes
Cardamoms
Cloves
Root ginger
Bay leaf
Peppercorns

Dumplings
Oatmeal
Flour
Suet
Egg

158

Provençal Bacon or Ham Casserole

3 lb/1.5 kg
boned and rolled ham or bacon roast
3 tablespoons dripping(s)
12 button onions
12 small carrots
4 leeks
Stock or beer
Sprig of parsley
Sprig of thyme
3 bay leaves

Soak the roast in cold water for about 6 hours if smoked, 2 hours if unsmoked. Place in a saucepan, cover with cold water and bring to the boil. Simmer for half the cooking time. (Full cooking time is 20 minutes per lb/450 g and 20 minutes over.) Remove meat, skin and score the fat into squares. Melt dripping(s) in a large ovenproof casserole and fry whole onions and carrots and chopped leek until lightly browned. Add sufficient stock or beer to cover. Place the meat in the casserole and add the herbs. Cover and bake at 350°F/180°C/Gas Mark 4 for remaining cooking time. Ten minutes before it is ready, remove lid to brown, increasing oven temperature to 425°F/220°C/Gas Mark 7. If liked it can be served with parsley sauce made with the stock from the vegetables.

Savory Ham/Bacon Roll

½ lb/225 g ham or bacon pieces
2 cups/8 oz/225 g plain (all-purpose) flour
1 teaspoon baking powder
Salt and pepper
2 tablespoons shredded suet
⅓ cup/1½ oz/40 g stale breadcrumbs
1 teaspoon mixed herbs
2 teaspoons chopped parsley
1 medium onion
2 tablespoons margarine
Chopped parsley to garnish

Sift flour, baking powder and pepper into a bowl. Blend ham pieces with suet, mixing well. Sprinkle in breadcrumbs, herbs and parsley and add grated onion. Add salt sparingly in case ham is salty. Use a little cold water to bind ingredients to a dough that can be handled. Form into a short roll, wrap in greaseproof (wax) paper then in foil and tie at each end. Steam for about 2½ hours. Remove wrappings, place roll on hot dish and rub surface with small piece of margarine, afterward sprinkling with more chopped parsley. Serve with gravy or hot tomato sauce.

Farmhouse Ham/Bacon

2 lb/1 kg ham or bacon
1 lb/450 g cooking apples
2 cups/1 pint/500 ml cider
1 onion stuck with 4 cloves
Sprig of rosemary
2 teaspoons cornstarch

Topping
3 teaspoons French mustard
2 teaspoons sugar (preferably demerara)
Cloves

Place the meat in a saucepan and cover with cold water. Bring slowly to the boil, discard water. Peel and slice apples, place in saucepan with the cider, onion and rosemary. Place the meat on top. Cover and bring to the boil. When boiling reduce heat to a gentle simmer and cook for 20 minutes per lb/450 g and 20 minutes over. Remove the meat from the cooking juices and place it in a roasting pan. Mix mustard and sugar together. Remove rind and spread the mixture over the top fat, score the surface into diamond shapes and stick with cloves. Bake at 400°F/200°C/Gas Mark 6 for 10 minutes. Meanwhile drain the stock from the apples and reduce it to 1½ cups/¾ pint/375 ml. Blend cornstarch with cold water, add a little of the hot juices, return to the pan and boil to thicken the gravy. Purée the apples and onion, discarding the cloves, and serve as applesauce with the meat.

NOTE

In Europe there is a type of pig especially reared to produce certain proportions of lean meat to fat. The roasts and cuts of meat coming from this pig are called **Bacon** or **Gammon** joints and are generally **not available in countries outside Europe**. In these countries **cooked or uncooked, smoked or unsmoked ham or picnic shoulder may be substituted** where indicated in these recipes.

Bacon Loaf

6 slices of bacon (streaky)
1½ lb/675 g lean bacon
1 small onion
½ cup/2 oz/50 g breadcrumbs
2 tablespoons chopped parsley
2 teaspoons sage
2 eggs
4 tablespoons stock
¼ teaspoon pepper

Remove any rind from the slices of bacon, and smooth out the bacon into thin slices with a flat-bladed knife. Line 1 lb/450 g loaf pan with these bacon slices. Cut the lean bacon in pieces and mince finely with the onion. Mix with the breadcrumbs, parsley, sage, eggs, stock and pepper and put into the bacon-lined pan. Cover with foil and stand the container in a roasting pan surrounded by water. Bake at 325°F/170°C/Gas Mark 3 for 1¼ hours. Cool in the pan with weights on top and turn out when completely cold.

Bacon Maryland

Illustrated on pages 172/173

8 slices back bacon
Prepared mustard
4 bananas
Oil
¾ cup/3 oz/75 g grated cheese
2 tablespoons butter
8 oz/225 g can of corn kernels
1 can of red pepper
Salt and pepper

Spread the bacon lightly with butter. Cut the bananas into halves and dip them in oil. Wrap each piece of banana in a strip of bacon. Secure with toothpicks. Grill (broil) for 4 minutes. Turn the bacon and banana rolls and sprinkle with grated cheese. Grill (broil) again for 3 minutes. Melt the butter and add the drained corn and chopped red pepper. Heat through and season well. Spoon the corn mixture onto a serving dish and top with the banana and bacon rolls. Serve with a salad.

Bacon/Ham Carbonnade

1 lb/450 g shoulder bacon (in one piece)
or picnic shoulder
2 tablespoons lard
2 onions
1 garlic clove
½ cup/2 oz/50 g seasoned flour
1 cup/½ pint/250 ml ale
½ cup/¼ pint/125 ml water
Sprig of parsley
Sprig of thyme
1 bay leaf
Few drops of Tabasco sauce
Strip of lemon peel
3 cups/10 oz/300 g button mushrooms

Melt the lard and fry the chopped onion and crushed garlic until soft and golden. Cut the shoulder into 1-in/2.5-cm squares and toss in the seasoned flour. Add to the onions and cook for 5 minutes. Add the ale, water, herbs, Tabasco sauce, lemon peel and whole mushrooms. Bring to the boil, cover and simmer for 1¼ hours.

Midweek Stew

1½ lb/675 g bacon or ham roast
3 tablespoons butter
1 turnip
1 small parsnip
2 tablespoons plain (all-purpose) flour
1½ teaspoons dry mustard
2 cups/1 pint/500 ml stock

Remove the rind from the meat and cut it into 1-in/2.5-cm cubes. Put pieces in cold water, stir to separate the meat and bring slowly to the boil. Simmer for 10 minutes. Drain the meat well and keep on one side. Melt the butter, add the diced turnip and parsnip and cook slowly, stirring occasionally for 5 minutes. Stir in the flour and mustard slowly, cook for 1 minute and then gradually add the stock. Bring to the boil stirring and cook for 2 minutes. Add pepper to taste. Finally, add the meat, cover and cook slowly for 1 hour 15 minutes.

Bacon/Ham and Cider Hotpot

1½ lb/675 g smoked shoulder bacon
(in one piece) or picnic shoulder
1 smoked pork sausage
6 medium potatoes
2 medium onions
Salt and pepper
Cider to cover
1 cup/½ pint/250 ml cream
Chopped parsley

Cut meat into finger-shaped pieces. Cut sausage into chunks and slice onions into rings. Put all these ingredients with the whole potatoes and seasoning into an oven-proof casserole. Cover with cider and cook at 350°F/180°C/Gas Mark 4 for 1 hour, stirring occasionally, until shoulder is tender and potatoes are done. Stir in cream and chopped parsley just before serving.

Honey Roast Ham

Recipe on page 154

Boned, rolled unsmoked ham
Thick honey
Orange juice
Orange
Arrowroot

Bacon/Ham with Cranberry Sauce Glaze

Recipe on page 151

Boned bacon or ham roast
Cider
Water
Sugar
Cranberry sauce

Summer Bacon/ Ham Soup

1 knuckle smoked bacon (ham)
1 pig's trotter (foot)
Sprig of parsley
Sprig of thyme
1 bay leaf
10 black peppercorns
1 onion stuck with 4 cloves
4 cups/ 2 pints/ 1 liter water
$\frac{3}{4}$ lb/ 350 g mixed summer vegetables
(carrots, peas, beans, etc.)
$\frac{1}{3}$ cup/ 3 fl oz/ 75 ml sherry

Put the knuckle, trotter (foot) and all the seasonings into a pan with the water. Bring to the boil and simmer gently for 1$\frac{1}{2}$ hours. Strain and add the diced vegetables. Cook until tender. Add the sherry and bacon (ham) cut from the bone. Re-season and chill thoroughly. Serve with slices of cucumber on top.

NOTE

In Europe there is a type of pig especially reared to produce certain proportions of lean meat to fat. The roasts and cuts of meat coming from this pig are called **Bacon** or **Gammon** joints and are generally **not available in countries outside Europe**. In these countries **cooked or uncooked, smoked or unsmoked ham or picnic shoulder may be substituted** where indicated in these recipes.

Boiled Bacon/ Ham and Dumplings

3 lb/ 1.5 kg bacon or ham roast
1 lb/ 450 g onions
1 lb/ 450 g carrots
1 bay leaf
2 cloves

Dumplings
$\frac{3}{4}$ cup/ 3 oz/ 75 g
self-raising (self-rising) flour
$\frac{1}{4}$ cup/ 1 oz/ 25 g shredded suet
$\frac{1}{4}$ teaspoon salt
1 teaspoon mixed herbs

Put the meat into a pan of cold water. Bring to the boil and discard water. Cover with fresh cold water, bring to the boil and add sliced onions, carrots, bay leaf and cloves. Cover and simmer for 1 hour. Mix the flour, suet, salt and herbs and mix to a firm dough with cold water. Form into 8 balls. Drop into the pan with the meat and simmer for 20 minutes. Lift out the meat and strip off rind. Put on a serving dish and serve with the vegetables and dumplings. Parsley sauce is very good with this.

Boiled Ham/ Bacon with Stuffed Onions

2 lb/ 1 kg bacon or ham roast
4 medium onions
$\frac{2}{3}$ cup/ 2 oz/ 50 g mushrooms
1 teaspoon tomato purée
Salt and pepper
2 tablespoons butter

Put the meat into cold water, bring to the boil, and discard the water. Cover with fresh cold water, bring to the boil and simmer for 1 hour. Peel the onions and boil them for 10 minutes. Cut them in half and scoop out the center flesh. Chop the onion flesh and the mushrooms and mix with the tomato purée, salt and pepper. Fill the onion shells and dot the top of each with a little butter. Bake the onions at 350°F/ 180°C/ Gas Mark 4 for 20 minutes. When the meat is cooked, remove the rind and place it on a serving dish, surrounded by the stuffed onions. A hot tomato sauce is good with this dish.

Stuffed Gammon Rashers (Ham Steaks)

6 unsmoked gammon rashers or
thinly sliced ham steaks
1 small onion
$\frac{1}{2}$ lb/ 225 g spinach
$\frac{1}{4}$ lb/ 100 g pork sausagemeat
3 tablespoons fresh breadcrumbs
2 tablespoons lemon juice

Cook spinach and combine with the other ingredients. Mix thoroughly and season with salt and pepper. Spread a little of the mixture on each slice, roll up lengthways and secure with thread. Brown in hot oil. Transfer to casserole, pour in a little stock and cook covered at 375°F/ 190°C/ Gas Mark 5 for 45 minutes.

Stuffed Bacon/Ham Slices with Rice and Lemon Sauce

8 bacon collar rashers
(thinly cut fresh ham steaks)
Little fat for frying
1¼ cups/6 oz/175 g long-grain rice

Stuffing
2 tablespoons butter
1 onion
1 cup/2 oz/50 g fresh breadcrumbs
1 tablespoon chopped parsley
Grated rind of ½ lemon
Salt and pepper

Sauce
2 tablespoons butter
¼ cup/1 oz/25 g plain (all-purpose) flour
1 cup/½ pint/250 ml chicken stock
Grated rind and juice of ½ lemon

Remove rind (if any) and spread the slices on a board. Chop the onion finely, make up stuffing, and divide it among the rashers (slices). Roll them up neatly and tie each with string. Melt some fat and fry the stuffed meat slices until lightly brown all over, turning frequently. Reduce heat and cook for 10 minutes. Cook and drain the rice. Make the sauce by melting the butter, add the flour, cook 1 minute, then gradually stir in the stock. Bring to the boil stirring. Add lemon juice and rind and cook for 2 minutes. Serve the stuffed bacon slices on the rice and pass the sauce separately.

Bacon/Ham Bolognese

12 strips of bacon (streaky)
1 onion
1 tablespoon plain (all-purpose) flour
⅔ cup/2 oz/50 g mushrooms
14 oz/400 g can tomatoes
Pinch of mixed herbs
Salt and pepper
½ lb/225 g spaghetti

Remove rind (if any) and cut bacon into strips. Fry pieces slowly to extract some fat, then stir in the chopped onion and cook slowly for 5 minutes. Stir in the flour, mushrooms, tomatoes and herbs, bring to the boil, breaking up the tomatoes if necessary. Reduce heat and cook for 15 minutes, taste and add salt and pepper if required. Meanwhile cook the spaghetti in boiling salted water for 15 minutes until just tender. Drain well. Serve the spaghetti on a heated dish with the bacon bolognese spooned over.

Ham/Bacon Salad

8 slices cold ham (or boiled bacon)
4 heads endive
(called chicory in Great Britain)
3 small oranges
½ cup/1½ oz/40 g walnut halves
Maraschino cherries
Juice of ½ lemon
Juice of ½ orange
1 tablespoon clear honey
3 tablespoons oil

Split heads of endive in half lengthwise. Cut oranges into thin slices after peeling and removing all the white pith. Arrange endive and oranges round the edge of a flat plate and add walnut halves. Place slices of ham in the center and arrange cherries round the slices. Mix the fruit juices, honey and oil together and sprinkle over the salad.

Devilled Ham

4 ham steaks
A little melted butter
Prepared mustard
12 oz/350 g can pineapple slices
2 tablespoons sugar (preferably demerara)

Snip the edges of the ham steaks to prevent them curling under the grill (broiler). Brush one side with a little melted butter and cook them under a fairly hot grill (broiler) for 5 minutes. Turn the steaks over, brush with a little more butter and spread them with the mustard. Sprinkle with sugar. Grill (broil) for a further 5 minutes. Strain the juice from the pineapple and arrange 2 slices on each steak, sprinkle these with sugar and heat for a further 2 minutes to melt the sugar.

Bacon/Ham Patties

½ lb/225 g cooked bacon or ham roast
1 medium onion
½ cup/2 oz/50 g breadcrumbs
1 tablespoon chopped parsley
½ teaspoon mixed herbs
2 eggs
Pepper
¼ cup/2 oz/50 g butter

Grind the meat and onion and add the remaining ingredients. Mix well and shape into cakes on a lightly floured board. Melt butter and fry gently for 10-15 minutes turning once. Serve with vegetables or salad, or in soft rolls.

Ham and Leek Pie

Recipe on page 167

Cooked ham
Lard
Margarine
Flour
Salt and pepper
Milk
Leeks
Butter
Stuffed green olives
Eggs
Ground mace

Bacon/Ham in Cider

2 lb/ 1 kg ham or bacon roast
1 cup/ ½ pint/ 250 ml cider or beer
1 small onion
1 carrot
Sprig of parsley
Sprig of thyme
1 bay leaf
2 peppercorns
Toasted breadcrumbs

(If too salty bring the meat to the boil in cold water and drain.) Place the meat in cider or beer and enough water to cover. Add onion, carrot, herbs and peppercorns. Bring back to the boil, reduce heat and simmer gently for 20 minutes per lb/ 450 g and 20 minutes over. Drain the meat, remove string and rind. Coat with toasted breadcrumbs. Serve cold with salad.

Savory Ham and Apple Pudding

2 cups/ 8 oz/ 225 g
self-raising (self-rising) flour
1 teaspoon salt
½ teaspoon dry mustard
1 cup/ 4 oz/ 100 g shredded suet
½ cup/ ¼ pint/ 125 ml cold water

Filling
1 lb/ 450 g ham
¼ lb/ 4 oz/ 100 g cabbage heart
1 large onion
½ lb/ 225 g cooking apples
2 tablespoons molasses
Pepper to taste

Chop meat, cabbage, onion and apples. Mix all filling ingredients together. Into another bowl sift flour and salt together. Add suet and toss all together. Mix into a stiff dough with the water. Roll out two-thirds of dough to line a well-greased pudding basin (steaming mold). Fill with ham and vegetable mixture and cover with lid made by rolling out the rest of the dough. Cover with greased foil and steam steadily for 3 hours.

Bacon/Ham Soufflé

6 oz/ 175 g cooked bacon or ham roast
2 tablespoons butter
1 tablespoon grated onion
¼ cup/ 1 oz/ 25 g plain (all-purpose) flour
½ cup/ ¼ pint/ 125 ml milk
3 eggs
Salt and pepper
1 tablespoon chopped parsley

Heat oven to 350°F/ 180°C/ Gas Mark 4. Lightly butter a 7-in/ 17.5-cm soufflé dish. Chop the bacon (ham) finely. Melt the butter, add the onion and cook for 2 minutes. Add the flour, stir round and gradually add the milk, beat well and bring to the boil, cook for 2 minutes. Remove pan from the heat. Stir in the bacon. Separate the egg yolks from the whites, adding the yolks to the pan. Beat well, add salt, pepper and parsley. Beat the whites until stiff and dry. Using a metal spoon fold evenly into the mixture. Pour into prepared dish and cook for 45 minutes until the mixture is set and firm to the touch. Serve at once.

NOTE

In Europe there is a type of pig especially reared to produce certain proportions of lean meat to fat. The roasts and cuts of meat coming from this pig are called **Bacon** or **Gammon** joints and are generally **not available in countries outside Europe.** In these countries **cooked or uncooked, smoked or unsmoked ham or picnic shoulder may be substituted** where indicated in the following recipes.

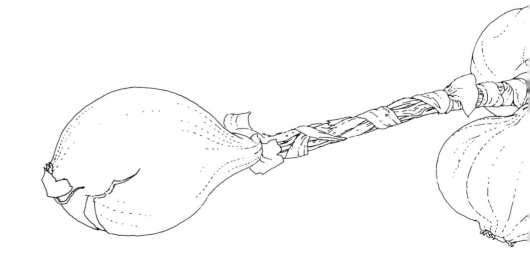

Bacon/Ham Stuffed Peppers

1½ lb/675 g cooked bacon or ham
3 red peppers
3 green peppers
¼ cup/2 oz/50 g butter
2 large onions
3 tablespoons plain (all-purpose) flour
1 cup/½ pint/250 ml milk
Salt and pepper
1 teaspoon Worcestershire sauce
1 cup/4 oz/100 g grated cheese
¾ cup/1½ oz/40 g fresh white breadcrumbs
1 egg yolk
Oil

Cut a thin slice from the stalk end of the peppers and remove the seeds. Cook in boiling salted water for 10 minutes and drain thoroughly. Melt butter in a pan and cook the finely chopped onions until soft. Stir in the flour and cook for a minute, then add the milk and bring to the boil. Simmer for 2 minutes, then add seasonings, cheese, breadcrumbs, chopped bacon and egg yolk. Fill peppers with this mixture and stand in a buttered ovenproof dish. Brush outside skins with oil and bake at 375°F/190°C/ Gas Mark 5 for 20 minutes.

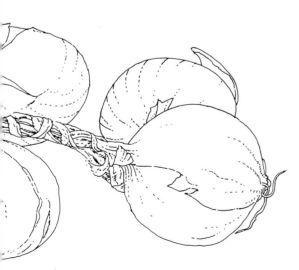

Ham in Pastry Parcels

½ lb/225 g ham steak
2 cups/8 oz/225 g puff pastry
⅔ cup/2 oz/50 g mushrooms
1 onion
1 egg
2 tablespoons butter
Tomato purée or ketchup

Divide the ham steak in half. Remove the rind (if any) and snip into the fat at ½ in/ 1.25 cm intervals. Chop mushrooms and onion and cook in a little butter until soft. Divide pastry in half and roll each half into a square. Place the ham pieces in the center. Spread a little purée or ketchup on top of each and cover with mushroom and onion mixture. Brush pastry edges with beaten egg. Fold pastry over carefully, sealing the joined edges. Place on a baking sheet and brush again with beaten egg. Bake at 425°F/ 220°C/Gas Mark 7 for 20 minutes until pastry is well risen. Lightly cover with foil and continue cooking for 15 minutes.

Ham Mousse

½ lb/225 g cooked ham
4 tablespoons horseradish sauce
2 tablespoons mayonnaise
½ teaspoon dry mustard
1 tablespoon gelatine
½ cup/¼ pint/125 ml water
½ cup/¼ pint/125 ml cream

Grind the ham or chop it very finely. Dissolve the gelatine in very hot (but not boiling) water. Cool. Combine with the cream and mayonnaise. Add the remaining ingredients, mixing thoroughly. Pour into a moistened mold and chill until set.

Ham and Leek Pie

Illustrated on pages 164/165

3 oz/75 g cooked ham (2 slices approx)
3 tablespoons lard
3 tablespoons margarine
1½ cups/6 oz/150 g plain (all-purpose) flour
¼ teaspoon salt
1 cup/½ pint/250 ml milk
2 leeks
2 tablespoons butter
⅓ cup/2 oz/50 g Spanish stuffed green olives
3 eggs
Pepper
Pinch of ground mace

Rub the lard and margarine into the flour and salt until the mixture resembles fine breadcrumbs. Add 1–2 tablespoons milk to mix to a firm dough. Roll out and line 9 in/ 22.5 cm pie plate. Line with foil and fill with baking beads and bake at 400°F/200°C/Gas Mark 6 for 15 minutes. Remove beads and foil and leave pie shell to cool slightly. Slice the leeks into rings and cook in the butter until soft but not colored. Arrange on the bottom of the pastry shell. Put diced ham and halved olives on top. Beat the eggs, add the pepper, mace and remaining milk and pour into the pie. Cook at 375°F/190°C/ Gas Mark 5 for 40 minutes until set. Serve hot or cold.

Ham Spread

1¾ cups/10 oz/300 g cooked ham
3 teaspoons horseradish sauce
¼ teaspoon ground black pepper
3 tablespoons white sauce
½ teaspoon curry powder

Grind the ham finely and add the other ingredients, mixing thoroughly. Season to taste and use as a spread.

Recipe on page 131

Pork and Bacon Loaf

Pork belly or flank
Unsmoked back bacon
White breadcrumbs
Onion
Dry mustard
Mixed herbs
Salt and pepper
Egg
Cider
(Olives optional)

Savory Brains

2 sets lamb's brains
1 cup/½ pint/250 ml stock
1 tablespoon vinegar
1 medium onion
2 tablespoons butter
2 tablespoons white wine
Salt and pepper
2 slices toasted bread
Paprika

Soak brains in cold salted water for 1 hour. Remove skin and any traces of blood. Drain and then simmer in stock and vinegar for 15 minutes. Drain and put the brains into very cold water. When cool, drain them well. Chop the onion and fry in butter until soft. Put to one side of the pan and add brains, broken into small pieces, to the fat. Fry until browned and then mix with the onion. Add the wine, salt and pepper and cook for 5 minutes. Serve on toasted bread with a sprinkling of paprika.

Brains à la Française

1 lb/450 g brains
2 pints/1 liter water
1 teaspoon salt
1 onion
2 tablespoons vinegar
Sprig of parsley
Sprig of thyme
1 bay leaf
Salt and pepper
A little flour
1 egg
Breadcrumbs
Oil for deep frying
Lemon wedges

Simmer brains with the water, salt, sliced onion, vinegar and herbs for 15 minutes. Cool and drain. Break into bite-sized pieces. Season the brains well with salt and pepper. Toss in flour then coat with beaten egg and breadcrumbs. Fry in hot oil for 5 minutes until crisp and golden, and drain. Serve with lemon wedges.

Liver and Bacon Pâté

6 slices of bacon (streaky) for lining
½ lb/225 g pig's liver
½ lb/225 g bacon (streaky)
1 garlic clove
1 large onion
¼ cup/2 oz/50 g butter
Salt and pepper
3 bay leaves

Sauce
1 cup/½ pint/250 ml milk
2 blades mace
1 bay leaf
8 peppercorns
2 tablespoons butter
¼ cup/1 oz/25 g plain (all-purpose) flour

Remove the rinds (if any) from the 6 bacon slices and stretch each one on a board with the back of a knife. Lay the bacon at the bottom and round the sides of a greased terrine or straight-sided dish. Fry liver, de-rinded ½ lb of bacon, garlic and roughly chopped onion in butter for 10 minutes. Grind or put into a blender. Put milk for sauce into a pan with mace, bay leaf and peppercorns. Bring very slowly to the boil, leave to stand for 10 minutes, then strain. Melt butter in pan, add flour and cook for 1 minute. Remove from heat and gradually stir in milk. Return to heat and bring to the boil, stirring all the time until sauce bubbles and thickens. Add to liver mixture and blend well. Season to taste. Turn into prepared dish and top with bay leaves. Cover with foil and lid. Stand in a roasting pan of hot water and bake for 1 hour at 350°F/180°C/Gas Mark 4. Allow to become quite cold. Serve with toast.

Liver and Potato Casserole

¾ lb/350 g liver
1½ lb/675 g potatoes
6 bacon slices
1 cup/½ pint/250 ml stock or water
2 tablespoons plain (all-purpose) flour
4 medium onions
Salt and pepper
Dripping(s)

Cut the liver into small pieces. Dip into flour seasoned with salt and pepper, and brown on each side in hot dripping(s). Remove from the pan, and fry the sliced onions until golden. Peel and slice the potatoes. Put layers of potatoes, onions, and liver in a casserole, seasoning well, and put the slices of bacon on top. Pour on stock to come halfway up the dish. Bake in a moderate oven at 375°F/190°C/Gas Mark 5 for 1 hour.

Stuffed Liver

1½ lb/675 g pig's liver
2 hard-boiled eggs
2 teaspoons parsley
8 slices of bacon
2 tablespoons butter
1 large onion
¼ cup/1 oz/25 g seasoned flour
1 cup/½ pint/250 ml beef stock

Wash and skin the liver. Cut into 8 large thin slices. Chop the hard-boiled eggs and mix with parsley. Put a spoonful on each slice of liver, and roll up. Roll a bacon strip round each parcel and secure with thread. Melt butter in ovenproof casserole, and lightly fry the chopped onion. Sprinkle on the flour. Pour the stock into the casserole, stir and bring to the boil. Put in the liver and bacon rolls. Cover and cook at 325°F/170°C/Gas Mark 3 for 1 hour.

Lancaster Liver Dumplings

1½ lb/675 g ox liver
¼ cup/2 oz/50 g butter
1 small onion
6 tablespoons dry breadcrumbs
2 eggs
¼ teaspoon salt
½ cup/2 oz/50 g plain (all-purpose) flour
1 teaspoon baking powder
Milk

Chop the liver coarsely and fry in half the butter until well done. Remove from the pan and chop finely. Heat the remaining butter and add ground onion and breadcrumbs, tossing until the onions are transparent. Beat eggs lightly, combine with liver and mix with onions and breadcrumbs. Add salt, flour, baking powder and enough milk to make mixture easy to roll into 1½ in/3.75 cm balls. Roll dumplings in additional flour and drop into lightly boiling soup, or a vegetable stew. Cover and cook for 30 minutes.

Liver and Bacon Casserole

1 lb/450 g liver
4 slices of lean bacon
2 cooking apples
2 large onions
1 cup/4 oz/100 g breadcrumbs
1 tablespoon chopped parsley
1 teaspoon salt
¼ teaspoon pepper
1 cup/½ pint/250 ml stock or water

Slice the liver, and cut the bacon into small pieces. Peel and chop apples and onions. Grease a casserole, put in a layer of liver, then bacon. Top with a layer of breadcrumbs, onion, parsley, salt and pepper, then apple. Repeat the layers, finishing with breadcrumbs, and pour in the stock or water. Bake at 375°F/190°C/Gas Mark 5 for 2 hours, removing the cover for the last 30 minutes.

Liver and Tomato Pudding

Pastry
2 cups/8 oz/225 g
self-raising (self-rising) flour
1 teaspoon salt
¾ cup/3 oz/75 g shredded suet
8 tablespoons cold water

Filling
1 lb/450 g lamb's liver
2 tablespoons plain (all-purpose) flour
1 tablespoon marjoram
2 tablespoons chopped parsley
1 medium onion
8 oz/225 g can tomatoes
2 tablespoons tomato purée
Salt and pepper

To make pastry sift together flour and salt. Add shredded suet and mix with water to a soft, but not sticky, dough. Turn out and knead lightly until smooth. Roll out into a circle approximately 12 in/30 cm in diameter, on a lightly floured surface, and cut out one-quarter from the circle for the lid. Line a 2 pint/1 liter pudding basin (steaming mold) with the larger piece of pastry, pinching cut edges together.

For filling, toss pieces of liver in flour, marjoram and parsley. Combine liver and onion and pack into pudding basin (steaming mold). Break up tomatoes in juice with a fork and mix with tomato purée, salt and pepper. Pour over the liver. Roll out remaining pastry to form a lid. Dampen edges of pastry and cover with pastry lid. Seal and trim edges. Cover loosely with greased greaseproof (wax) paper or foil. Steam in a pan of boiling water for 4 hours.

Liver and Kidney Envelope

½ lb/225 g chicken's livers
½ lb/225 g lamb's kidneys
2 cups/8 oz/225 g puff pastry
¼ cup/2 oz/50 g dripping(s)
1 medium onion
⅔ cup/2 oz/50 g mushrooms
1 teaspoon mixed herbs
1 tablespoon tomato chutney
1 tablespoon plain (all-purpose) flour
½ cup/¼ pint/125 ml stock
Salt and pepper

Fry finely chopped liver and kidneys in dripping(s) with chopped onion and sliced mushrooms. Add chutney, herbs and seasoning. Remove mixture from pan, leaving excess fat behind. Stir flour into pan, add stock and boil until reduced to a thick brown sauce. Return mixture to pan and leave until quite cold. Roll out pastry to a 12-in/30-cm square. Place mixture in center. Dampen edges. Fold up like an envelope. Seal edges and glaze. Bake 15 minutes at 425°F/200°C/Gas Mark 7, then reduce heat to 375°F/190°C/Gas Mark 5 for 30 minutes. Serve hot or cold.

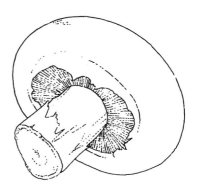

Bacon Maryland

Recipe on page 159

Back bacon
Mustard
Bananas
Oil
Grated cheese
Butter
Corn kernels
Canned red pepper
Salt and pepper

Mock Goose

1 lb/450 g liver
2 lb/1 kg potatoes
1 tablespoon plain (all-purpose) flour
Salt and pepper
2 onions
1 apple
1 teaspoon sage
1½ cups/¾ pint/375 ml
boiling stock or water

Wash and peel the potatoes and cut in slices. Wipe the liver with a damp cloth and cut in slices ½ in/1.25 cm thick. Mix the flour, salt and pepper together and coat the liver with this mixture. Peel and chop the onions finely, peel and chop the apple. Mix together the onion, apple and sage. Grease a casserole and put in layers of potato, liver and onion, seasoning well between each layer and making the top layer potato. Pour over the boiling stock or water and cover with well greased paper and a lid. Bake at 350°F/180°C/Gas Mark 4 for 1 hour. Remove the lid and paper and return it to the oven for a further 20 minutes to brown the potatoes on top.

Baked Stuffed Liver

1½ lb/675 g liver
¼ cup/1 oz/25 g plain (all-purpose) flour
9 slices of bacon
2 tablespoons breadcrumbs
1 teaspoon chopped parsley
½ teaspoon salt
¼ teaspoon pepper
1 small onion
¼ teaspoon grated lemon rind
1 cup/½ pint/250 ml stock

Toss liver in flour and put into a shallow baking pan or oven dish. Mix together breadcrumbs, parsley, salt and pepper, finely chopped onion and lemon rind, and moisten with a little stock. Spread over liver and top with a slice of bacon. Pour on stock and bake at 375°F/180°C/Gas Mark 5 for 35 minutes.

Baked Lamb's Liver

2 lb/1 kg lamb's liver
2 teaspoons olive oil
2 tablespoons butter
2 bay leaves
3 sage leaves
1 teaspoon black pepper
Salt
1 tablespoon whisky or brandy

Heavily butter the bottom and sides of an ovenproof dish. Put the 2 bay leaves in the bottom. Place liver in dish. Sprinkle the sage and pepper and oil on top. Bake at 350°F/180°C/Gas Mark 4 for 25 minutes until the liver is pink in the center and brown outside. Pour over heated and flamed whisky or brandy and serve.

Liver Crumble

¾ lb/350 g liver
6 slices of bacon
2 leeks
1 cup/7 fl oz/175 ml stock
1½ cups/6 oz/175 g plain (all-purpose) flour
⅓ cup/3 oz/75 g butter
¾ cup/3 oz/75 g Cheddar cheese
Chopped parsley

Cut the liver in thin slices. Gently fry the liver, then the bacon and finally the sliced leeks. Place in layers in an ovenproof dish and pour in the stock. Rub the butter into the flour until it looks like breadcrumbs. Crumble in the cheese and mix. Use the mixture to cover ingredients in the dish. Bake at 400°F/200°C/Gas Mark 6 for 35 minutes until the top is golden. Sprinkle with chopped parsley.

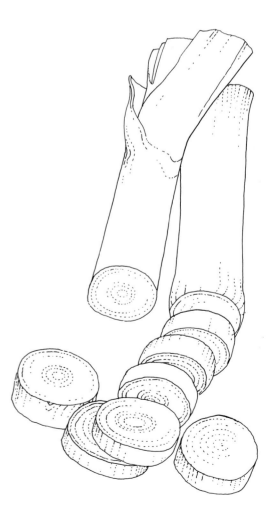

Liver and Olive Pâté

Illustrated on pages 180/181

12 slices of bacon
$\frac{1}{2}$ lb/225 g chicken's livers
1 lb/450 g pig's liver
$\frac{1}{2}$ lb/225 g chuck steak
1$\frac{1}{4}$ lb/550 g belly pork
$\frac{3}{4}$ lb/350 g fatty bacon
3 garlic cloves
1 tablespoon fresh chopped herbs
3 teaspoons salt
$\frac{3}{4}$ teaspoon ground mace
1 egg
2$\frac{1}{2}$ fl oz/65 ml sherry
4 tablespoons brandy
$\frac{2}{3}$ cup/3 oz/75 g Spanish stuffed green olives
Black pepper

Line two well-greased 1$\frac{1}{2}$ lb/675 g loaf pans or ovenproof dishes with the bacon. Heat oven to 300°F/150°C/Gas Mark 2. Mince (grind) the chicken's livers, pig's liver, beef, belly pork and fatty bacon. Crush garlic and add with all the other ingredients. Mix well to blend evenly. Put into the two prepared pans or dishes and cover with kitchen foil. Stand dishes in a roasting pan, containing about 1 in/2.5 cm of water. Cook for 2 hours. Remove from water and allow to cool. Turn out before serving.

Simple Liver Pâté

1 lb/450 g liver
12 slices of fatty bacon
Salt and pepper
Pinch of ground nutmeg
6 bacon slices

Remove the skin and nerves from the liver and chop and mince (grind) the meat finely. Trim and grind the fatty bacon. Season the meat well and mix together evenly. Line a terrine or shallow dish with thin slices of bacon. Fill with the ground meat and cover with the remaining bacon slices. Cover with well buttered paper and cook at 350°F/180°C/Gas Mark 4 (standing terrine in a baking pan containing about 2 in/5 cm boiling water) for 1 hour. Lift from the oven and leave to cool with a weight on top to give a firm pâté. Turn out and serve with hot toast.

Spanish Liver

$\frac{3}{4}$ lb/350 g liver
1 small onion
1 garlic clove
1 small green pepper
1 tablespoon oil
$\frac{1}{2}$ cup/$\frac{1}{4}$ pint/125 ml stock
2 teaspoons tomato purée
1 teaspoon chopped parsley
Salt and pepper

Fry the finely chopped onion, crushed garlic and chopped green pepper gently in oil for 10 minutes until soft. Add the diced liver and continue to fry gently, turning frequently until brown on all sides. Mix stock and tomato purée together. Add to mixture in frying pan and add parsley and seasoning. Simmer for 5 minutes. Serve with boiled rice or creamed potatoes.

Creamed Liver

1 lb/450 g lamb's liver
2 tablespoons butter
1 onion
2 tablespoons seasoned flour
1$\frac{1}{4}$ cups/4 oz/100 g button mushrooms
$\frac{1}{2}$ cup/$\frac{1}{4}$ pint/125 ml beef stock
4 tomatoes
2 tablespoons ketchup
Salt and pepper
$\frac{1}{2}$ cup/$\frac{1}{4}$ pint/125 ml sour cream

Melt butter in pan and fry chopped onion gently for 3 minutes. Cut slices of liver into $\frac{1}{4}$-in/0.75-cm thick strips and coat with seasoned flour. Add to pan with mushrooms and fry for 5 minutes, stirring occasionally. Add stock and bring to boil, stirring. Stir in skinned and quartered tomatoes and ketchup, season to taste and simmer for 2 minutes. Stir in sour cream and reheat without boiling. Serve with pasta or rice.

Saturday Bacon/ Ham Bake

¾ lb/350 g
cooked bacon collar (picnic shoulder)
1 lb/450 g potatoes
¼ cup/2 oz/50 g butter
½ cup/2 oz/50 g plain (all-purpose) flour
2 cups/1 pint/500 ml milk
2¼ cups/6 oz/150 g mushrooms
3 hard-boiled eggs
8 Spanish stuffed green olives
Salt and pepper
½ cup/2 oz/50 g Cheddar cheese

Boil the potatoes in their skins until just cooked. Drain, peel and slice. Cut the meat into neat cubes. Melt the butter, add the flour and cook for 2 minutes. Stir in the milk and bring to the boil. Add the mushrooms and simmer for 5 minutes. Add the potatoes, meat and chopped eggs. Stir in the sliced olives and season well. Turn into a large shallow ovenproof dish, sprinkle with grated cheese and grill until golden brown and hot.

Spanish Hot Meat Loaf

Recipe on page 131

Minced/ground pork
Minced/ground beef
Pork sausagemeat
White bread
Parsley
Tomato purée
Salt and pepper
Eggs
Stuffed green olives
Can of ratatouille or peperonata

Liver and Bacon Vol-au-Vent

6 slices of bacon
$\frac{3}{4}$ lb / 350 g lamb's liver
3 cups / 12 oz / 350 g puff pastry
1 egg to glaze
2 tablespoons butter or margarine
1 large onion
2 tablespoons plain (all-purpose) flour
1 cup / $\frac{1}{2}$ pint / 250 ml beef stock
1 tablespoon Worcestershire sauce
2 medium tomatoes
Salt and pepper

Roll out pastry 16 × 8 in / 40 × 20 cm. Cut in half to form two squares. Brush edges of one square with milk. Cut out center of other square to within 1 in / 2.5 cm of edge, remove outer strip and place around edge of uncut square. Press down gently to seal. Flake and flute edges. Place on a damp baking tray with remaining pastry square. Prick well all over and brush with egg. Bake at 425°F / 220°C / Gas Mark 7 for 25 minutes until golden brown. For filling, heat butter in pan, add chopped onion and bacon, and fry gently for 5 minutes. Add chopped liver and cook, stirring, until browned. Stir in flour and cook for 1 minute. Add stock, Worcestershire sauce, chopped tomatoes and seasoning. Bring to the boil, cover and simmer for 10 minutes. Check seasoning. Fill case with liver mixture and top with pastry lid.

Liver and Bacon Dip

$\frac{1}{2}$ lb / 225 g lamb's liver
6 slices of bacon
2 tablespoons butter
2 eggs
1 medium onion
Salt and pepper
8 tablespoons mayonnaise

Melt butter in frying pan and cook liver lightly on both sides until brown outside, but still pink inside. Put through a fine grinder. Grill (broil) or fry chopped bacon and crumble into small pieces. Boil eggs until hard. Chop onion finely and cook in pan juices from liver. Mix together ground liver, crumbled bacon, chopped eggs and chopped cooked onion with pan juices. Season well with salt and pepper and mix until thoroughly blended with mayonnaise. Pile into dish and serve with biscuits (crackers) or toast or fingers of crispbread.

Kidney and Bacon Hotpot

6 slices lean bacon
1$\frac{1}{2}$ lb / 675 g pig's kidneys
1 medium onion
2 tablespoons butter
1$\frac{1}{2}$ cups / $\frac{3}{4}$ pint / 375 ml beef stock
1 lb / 450 g can tomatoes
1$\frac{1}{4}$ cups / 4 oz / 100 g mushrooms

Chop the onion and bacon and fry together until lightly browned. Core and chop the kidneys and add to the pan with the butter. Fry for 3 minutes. Put into a casserole and cover with the stock. Cover and cook at 350°F / 180°C / Gas Mark 4 for 30 minutes. Add tomatoes and sliced mushrooms and cook for 15 minutes.

Kidney Casserole

1 lb / 450 g lamb's or veal kidneys
2 medium onions
2 tablespoons dripping(s)
4 slices of bacon
Flour
Salt and pepper
$\frac{1}{2}$ cup / $\frac{1}{4}$ pint / 125 ml stock

Clean the kidneys, skin and remove cores, and cut in slices. Chop the onions finely and fry in melted dripping(s) until golden. Put the onions in a casserole, arrange the kidneys on top, then pieces of chopped bacon. Season with salt and pepper and dust lightly with flour. Cover with stock and cook at 350°F / 180°C / Gas Mark 4 for 40 minutes.

Kidney Omelette

4 eggs
Salt and pepper
1 tablespoon butter

Filling
2 kidneys
1 beef stock cube
Salt and pepper
2 tablespoons butter
$\frac{1}{4}$ cup/ 1 oz/ 25 g plain (all-purpose) flour
$\frac{1}{2}$ cup/ $\frac{1}{4}$ pint/ 125 ml hot water

Prepare the kidneys by removing outer skin and washing them well. Slice and toss in the seasoned flour. Melt butter in a saucepan, put in the kidneys and fry for a few minutes. Add the rest of the flour and the stock cube crumbled and dissolved in the hot water. Bring to the boil and stir continuously. Beat up the eggs and season. Melt butter in an omelette pan and pour in the egg mixture. When it starts to set, tilt the pan so that the uncooked mixture runs to the sides. When the omelette is set, fill with the kidney sauce, fold in half and turn out on dish.

Devilled Kidney Ramekins

6 lamb's kidneys
$1\frac{1}{2}$ lb/ 675 g mashed potatoes
3 teaspoons butter
1 tablespoon cream
6 tomatoes
4 ham slices
Salt and pepper
Prepared mustard
2 bacon slices (cut into 6)

Cream potatoes well, adding butter, cream (or top of milk), and a dash of pepper. Line ramekins thickly with potato mixture, piping a little through a coarse icing nozzle to make a ribbon of potato cream around top edges. Cut a slice from each tomato and scoop out seeds. Drain well and dust insides with pepper and salt. Skin and core kidneys. Cut bacon into small pieces and fry until crisp. Divide pieces between the tomato cups. Fry or grill (broil) kidneys lightly and spread with a little mustard before putting the halves together and fitting them into the tomato cups. Put a small square of ham over each and bake at 400°F/ 200°C/ Gas Mark 6 until ham is crisped and contents of dishes piping hot.

Kidney and Liver Pudding

$\frac{1}{2}$ lb/ 225 g ox kidney
$\frac{1}{2}$ lb/ 225 g sheep's liver
6 slices/ 4 oz/ 100 g bacon
1 tablespoon plain (all-purpose) flour
Salt and pepper
Ground nutmeg
Ground mace
1 cup/ $\frac{1}{2}$ pint/ 250 ml beef stock
2 cups/ 8 oz/ 225 g
self-raising (self-rising) flour
1 cup/ 4 oz/ 100 g shredded suet

Wash the kidneys and liver well, dry them and cut into small pieces. Remove the rind from the bacon and cut into pieces. Cook the bacon for a few minutes in a hot frying pan, then lift out and drain. Mix the flour and spices together and coat the pieces of liver and kidney. Fry them in the fat remaining from the bacon, adding a little dripping(s) if necessary. When the meat is nicely browned lift onto a plate and mix with the bacon. Mix the flour and suet and make into a soft dough with cold water. Cut one-third of the suet pastry for the top and roll out the remainder into a circle to line a greased $1\frac{1}{2}$ pint/ 750 ml pudding basin (steaming mold). Fill up with the meat, and add $\frac{1}{2}$ cup/ $\frac{1}{4}$ pint/ 125 ml stock. Cover with a round of suet crust pastry and seal the edges of the pastry together. Cover the pudding with greased paper and steam gently for $2\frac{1}{2}$–3 hours. Turn the pudding out of the basin onto a hot plate.

Creamed Kidneys

4 pig's kidneys
$\frac{1}{4}$ cup/2 oz/50 g butter
1$\frac{1}{4}$ cups/4 oz/100 g mushrooms
Salt and pepper
1 teaspoon cornstarch
1 tablespoon water
$\frac{1}{2}$ cup/$\frac{1}{4}$ pint/125 ml whipping cream
$\frac{1}{3}$ cup/3 fl oz/75 ml whisky
Fried or toasted bread

Cut the kidneys and remove cores. Melt the butter and fry the mushrooms and kidneys for 3 minutes. Season and cover pan with lid. Cook gently for 10 minutes. Thicken with the cornstarch blended with 1 tablespoon water and bring to the boil. Add the cream just before serving. Turn onto a serving dish lined with fried or toasted bread. Add warmed whisky and set alight. Serve immediately.

Kidney Soup

$\frac{1}{2}$ lb/225 g ox kidney
2 tablespoons butter
1 small onion
4 cups/2 pints/1 liter stock
1 carrot
Sprig of parsley
Sprig of thyme
1 bay leaf
Salt and pepper
3 tablespoons cornstarch
2 tablespoons sherry

Wash the kidney and cut in slices. Cook in the butter for 1 minute and then add the sliced onion. Cook until the onion is soft and golden. Add the stock, chopped carrot, herbs, salt and pepper, cover and simmer for 1$\frac{1}{2}$ hours. Put through a sieve or blend in a liquidizer and return to the pan. Thicken with cornstarch blended in a little water and simmer for 5 minutes. Stir in sherry just before serving.

Kidneys in Wine

16 lamb's kidneys
2$\frac{1}{2}$ cups/8 oz/225 g mushrooms
$\frac{1}{4}$ cup/2 oz/50 g butter
1 cup/$\frac{1}{2}$ pint/250 ml red wine
Salt and pepper

Remove skin, fat and tubes from kidneys, and cut the kidneys in half. Cook gently in butter until just golden but still soft. Add sliced mushrooms, wine, salt and pepper and simmer for 30 minutes. Serve on toasted or fried bread, or with vegetables. For a more substantial dish, add 6 slices/4 oz/100 g cubed and fried bacon and $\frac{1}{2}$ lb/225 g fried chipolata sausages, cut in half. Simmer them in the wine with the kidneys.

Grilled (Broiled) Kidneys

8 sheep's kidneys
2 tablespoons melted butter
Salt and pepper
$\frac{1}{2}$ cup/4 oz/100 g butter
2 teaspoons finely chopped parsley
1 tablespoon lemon juice

Skin kidney and cut almost in half lengthwise. Skewer each one to remain open and keep their shape. Brush liberally with butter and grill (broil) on both sides. Season with salt and pepper. Cream the butter with parsley and lemon juice. Form into a cylinder shape and refrigerate until firm. Just before serving, cut parsley butter into slices and put a piece onto each kidney.

Liver and Olive Pâté

Recipe on page 175

Bacon
Chicken livers
Pig's liver
Chuck steak
Belly pork
Fatty bacon
Garlic
Chopped herbs
Salt
Ground mace
Egg
Sherry
Brandy
Stuffed green olives
Black pepper

Tongue Mold

6 lamb's tongues
3-hard-boiled eggs
5 teaspoons gelatine
1½ cups/¾ pint/375 ml chicken stock
Salt and pepper
1 cooked carrot

Gently simmer the tongues about 3 hours, until the skin comes away easily. Remove skin, halve the tongues lengthwise and leave to cool. Dissolve the gelatine in 2 tablespoons stock and when nearly cool add it to the remaining stock. Season well, adding a little cayenne pepper if desired. Wet a fancy mold or a round dish with cold water. Set a ¼ in/0.75 ml layer of stock first, then in the center of the base place a slice of egg. Cut carrot in shapes, place around egg and cover with a little of the stock. Leave to set. Place a ring of egg slices on first layer, cover with more stock, leave to set. Lay in the tongues either in halves or sliced as preferred, top with the remaining egg slices and pour in the rest of the stock, which should be enough to cover all the ingredients. Leave in a cold place to set. Chill until set and remove from mold to serve.

Lamb Tongues in Sweet and Sour Sauce

4 lamb's tongues
3 cups/1½ pints/675 ml stock
Salt and pepper
2 tablespoons cornstarch
½ cup/¼ pint/125 ml cider
2 tablespoons brown sugar
1 tablespoon cranberry sauce
1 tablespoon soy sauce
2 tablespoons vinegar

Soak the tongues in cold salted water for 2 hours. Drain and put into a pan with the stock and seasoning. Cover and simmer gently until cooked. Skin the tongues and remove any waste. Cut in half lengthwise and reheat in stock. Meanwhile, mix the cornstarch with a little of the cider. Put into a pan with the rest of the cider, sugar, cranberry sauce and soy sauce. Bring slowly to the boil, stirring well and simmer for 5 minutes. Add the vinegar. Drain the tongues and arrange on a bed of cooked noodles or other pasta. Cover with the sauce.

Glazed Lamb's Tongues

6 lamb's tongues
1½ cups/¾ pint/375 ml beef stock
1 carrot
1 turnip
1 onion
1 teaspoon brown sugar
Juice of ½ lemon
1 lb/450 g potatoes
2 tablespoons butter

Soak the tongues in a bowl of cold salt water for 2 hours. Dry them, then put in a casserole with the beef stock and the vegetables. Simmer gently for 1½ hours, until tender. Cook the potatoes then drain and mash with butter. Remove the tongues from the stock and remove the skin and trim the roots. Cut the tongues into 2 lengthwise and place on a hot dish. Skim any fat from the stock and reduce to a thick syrup-like glaze. Add the sugar and lemon juice and coat the tongues with the glaze. Arrange a border of potato round the tongues and serve at once.

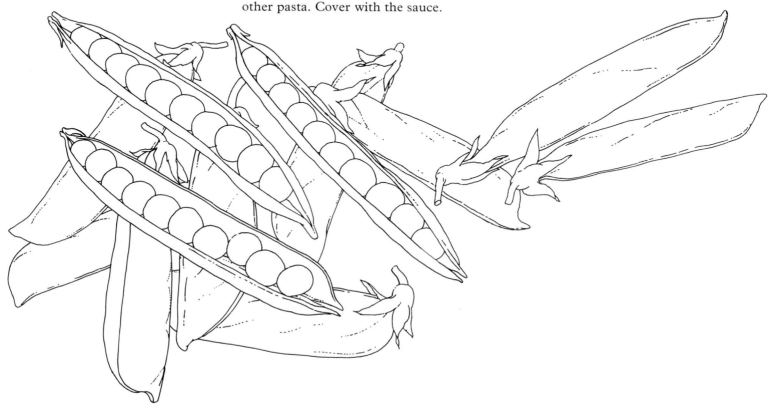

Pressed Ox Tongue

1 pickled ox tongue
1 onion
2 carrots
2 celery sticks
2 bay leaves
6 peppercorns

Wash the tongue well and soak overnight in plenty of cold water. Drain and put into a large pan with cold water to cover. Bring to the boil and boil for 5 minutes. Drain off this water. Cover the tongue with fresh cold water and add whole vegetables, bay leaves and peppercorns. Bring to the boil, cover and simmer gently until tender, removing scum from time to time. When cooked, remove tongue from pan and plunge into cold water for a minute or two so that it is cool enough to handle. Skin tongue, remove bones and waste from root end. Shape the tongue in a coil and place in a container just big enough to hold it and press under a very heavy weight. Leave in the refrigerator overnight, and remove from container to serve.

Tripe and Mushrooms

1 lb/450 g tripe
2 tablespoons vinegar
2 tablespoons olive oil
¼ cup/2 oz/50 g butter
1 small onion
¼ cup/1 oz/25 g plain (all-purpose) flour
1 lb/450 g can tomatoes
Salt and pepper
1 cup/4 oz/100 g breadcrumbs
2½ cups/8 oz/225 g mushrooms

Cut tripe in strips and leave in vinegar and oil for 30 minutes. Slice mushrooms thinly, and chop onion finely. Heat butter and brown onion, then cook mushrooms for 5 minutes. Blend in flour, then add tomatoes and cook till sauce thickens. Grease a casserole and put in a layer of tripe. Pour on tomato and mushroom mixture, and sprinkle on half of the breadcrumbs, salt and pepper. Add another layer of tripe, then sauce, and finish with breadcrumbs. Dot with butter, and bake without a lid for 20 minutes at 400°F/200°C/Gas Mark 6.

Tripe Rolls

1 lb/450 g tripe
8 slices of bacon
3 onions
3 carrots
Salt and pepper
Ground nutmeg
Bunch of mixed herbs
2 cups/1 pint/500 ml cider

Cut tripe in narrow slices, and put a bacon strip on each slice. Sprinkle with salt and pepper, a pinch of nutmeg and of mixed herbs. Roll up the slices, and secure with thread. Slice onions and carrots into a casserole, put the tripe rolls on top, cover with cider, and put on lid. Cook at 325°F/170°C/Gas Mark 3 for 3 hours.

Normandy Tripe

2 lb/1 kg tripe
1 cowheel
2 carrots
2 onions
3 leeks
3 whole cloves
Sprig of thyme
1 bay leaf
Salt and pepper
Cider

Cut tripe and cowheel in small pieces. Peel and slice carrots and onions, and clean and slice leeks. Put alternate layers of tripe, cowheel and vegetables in a casserole, seasoning well with salt and pepper. Tuck in cloves, thyme and bay leaf halfway up casserole. Put in cider to come halfway up layers. Cover and cook at 350°F/180°C/Gas Mark 4 for 3 hours. Just before serving, remove bones of cowheel, and color liquid with a little brown sugar.

Tripe Catalan

1 lb/450 g dressed tripe
2 tablespoons butter
1 large onion
4 tomatoes
1 garlic clove
1 teaspoon mixed herbs
1 teaspoon chopped parsley
Pinch of grated nutmeg
Salt and pepper
½ cup/¼ pint/125 ml white wine

Simmer the tripe in water until tender. Drain and cut into fine strips. Melt butter and cook finely sliced onion until soft and golden. Add the tripe. Skin the tomatoes and chop them. Add to the tripe with the crushed garlic, herbs, parsley, nutmeg, salt and pepper. Cook for 5 minutes. Add wine, cover and simmer until tender.

Sausage and Vegetable Brunch

Recipe on page 147

Cooked sausages
Onion
Red pepper
Oil
Garlic
Cooked peas
Eggs

Thick Oxtail Soup

1 lb / 450 g oxtail
2 tablespoons dripping(s)
1 large onion
1 carrot
1 small turnip
1 small leek
2 teaspoons plain (all-purpose) flour
2 teaspoons tomato purée
Sprig of parsley
Sprig of thyme
1 bay leaf
Salt and pepper
7 cups / 3½ pints / 2 liters water
2 tablespoons cornstarch
⅓ cup / 3 fl oz / 75 ml sherry or red wine

Cut the oxtail into pieces. Melt the dripping(s) and brown the oxtail. Remove the meat. Cut the onion, carrot and turnip in halves and chop the leek and brown them lightly in the fat. Return the meat to the pan and stir in the flour, tomato purée, herbs, salt and pepper. Mix well and pour in boiling water. Cover and simmer for 4 hours. Leave until cold and skim off the fat. Take the meat from the bones and cut into small pieces. Remove any large or unwieldy chunks of vegetables. Put the meat back into the soup and bring back to the boil. Mix the cornstarch with a little water and stir into the soup. Simmer for 5 minutes and stir in sherry or wine just before serving.

Oxtail Ragout

1 oxtail cut into 2 in / 5 cm pieces
½ cup / 2 oz / 50 g plain (all-purpose) flour
1 teaspoon salt
Pepper
Pinch of ground nutmeg
2 tablespoons oil
2 medium onions
2 carrots
2 turnips
1½ cups / ¾ pint / 375 ml beef stock
½ cup / ¼ pint / 125 ml red wine
2 bay leaves
12 Spanish stuffed green olives

Trim off any excess fat from the pieces. Combine flour, seasoning and nutmeg in a polythene bag. Put in oxtail and shake until coated. Heat oil in pan. Fry oxtail until golden all over and put into casserole. Fry sliced onions, carrots and turnips for 5 minutes without coloring. Add remaining flour and cook for a further minute. Add to casserole with stock, wine and bay leaves. Cover and cook at 300°F / 150°C / Gas Mark 2 for 4 hours, stirring occasionally. Add olives just before serving.

Crumbed Sweetbreads

1 lb / 450 g lamb's sweetbreads
1 cup / ½ pint / 250 ml water
Juice of ½ lemon
1 egg
4 tablespoons breadcrumbs
1 tablespoon chopped parsley
Salt and pepper
¼ cup / 2 oz / 50 g butter

Wash the sweetbreads and soak in cold water for 1 hour. Drain and put into a pan with 1 cup / ½ pint / 250 ml cold water and the lemon juice. Cover and simmer for 15 minutes. Drain and remove sinews and outside membranes. Flatten sweetbreads between two weighted plates for 1 hour. Dip sweetbreads in beaten egg and coat with breadcrumbs and parsley, season well. Fry gently in butter and serve with lemon wedges.

Sweetbread and Cider Casserole

1 lb / 450 g calf's or lamb's sweetbreads
1 onion
1¼ cups / 4 oz / 100 g mushrooms
2 tablespoons butter
¼ cup / 1 oz / 25 g plain (all-purpose) flour
1 cup / ½ pint / 250 ml cider
½ cup / ¼ pint / 125 ml milk
Salt and pepper

Put the sweetbreads into a pan of cold water and bring to the boil. Discard the water. Cover the sweetbreads in fresh water with a pinch of salt and simmer for 20 minutes. Skin the sweetbreads. Arrange the sweetbreads in layers in a casserole with sliced onion and mushrooms. Melt the butter, stir in the flour and cook for 1 minute. Gradually stir in cider and milk and bring to the boil. Simmer until thick and creamy and season to taste. Pour over the sweetbreads, cover and cook at 350°F / 180°C / Gas Mark 4 for 1 hour.

Braised Sweetbreads

2 pairs sweetbreads
1 onion
1 carrot
2 celery sticks
Sprig of parsley
Sprig of thyme
1 bay leaf
1 cup/ ½ pint/ 250 ml stock
Salt and pepper
½ cup/ ¼ pint/ 125 ml whipping cream

Prepare the sweetbreads by removing any skin and nerves. Blanch by putting into boiling water, then rinse in cold water. The sweetbreads are now ready to cook. Put into a small pan or casserole with the vegetables, stock and seasoning. Cover with a lid and cook gently for 30 minutes. Remove the sweetbreads and keep hot while making the sauce. Strain the vegetables from the pan and add the cream to the stock. Bring to the boil, and stir until smooth. Slice the sweetbreads and coat with the sauce.

Heart and Vegetable Casserole

4 pig's or lamb's hearts
Seasoned flour
2 tablespoons butter
1 tablespoon oil
2 slices of bacon
1 large onion
1 carrot
⅔ cup/ 2 oz/ 50 g mushrooms
1 green pepper
½ cup/ ¼ pint/ 125 ml stock
½ cup/ ¼ pint/ 125 ml red wine
Sprig of parsley
Sprig of thyme
1 bay leaf
Salt and pepper

Wash hearts thoroughly in cold water. Trim away fat and waste and snip the wall dividing the center. Soak for an hour in clean, salted water. Rinse, drain, cut into rough 1-in/ 2.5-cm squares and dry thoroughly. Dip in seasoned flour and fry in hot butter and oil mixed. When lightly browned place in casserole and keep warm. Fry bacon and vegetables until lightly brown in remaining butter and oil, adding a little more if necessary. Add to hearts in casserole, pour in stock and wine and add herbs and seasoning. Cover and cook for 1 hour at 350°F/ 180°C/ Gas Mark 4. Remove herbs before serving.

Stuffed Hearts

4 lamb's hearts
1 cup/ ½ pint/ 250 ml stock
3 fl oz/ 75 ml sweet sherry

Stuffing
⅔ cup/ 2 oz/ 50 g cooked ham
1 cup/ 4 oz/ 100 g fresh breadcrumbs
1 tablespoon chopped parsley
Pinch of sage
Pinch of rosemary
Pinch of thyme
Salt and pepper
1 egg
Juice of ½ lemon

Wash hearts well in cold water. Remove outer skin and any waste from hearts. Cut dividing wall of each heart to make a cavity. Soak hearts for 45 minutes in cold salted water. Rinse well and drain. Dice ham and mix dry stuffing ingredients together. Bind with egg and lemon juice. Pack stuffing well into the hearts. Put into casserole, pour over stock and cover with a tight fitting lid. Baste hearts frequently while cooking at 325°F/ 170°C/ Gas Mark 3 for 1½ hours. Add sherry for last 30 minutes.

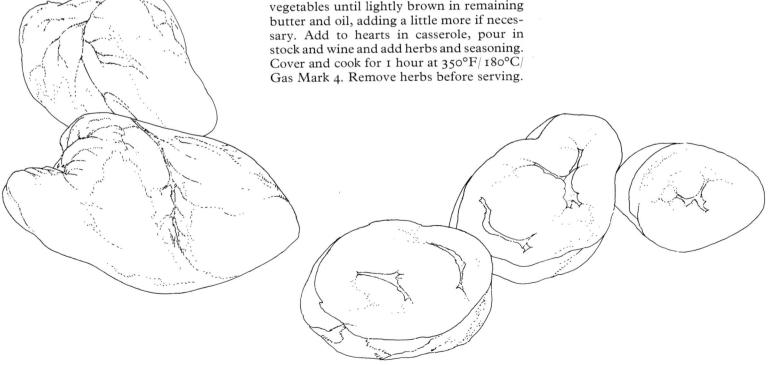

INDEX

numbers in *italic* type refer to illustrations

Acknowledgments

The author and publishers wish to
thank the following for their help and
advice in the preparation of this book
and for the use of photographs:
*MEAT (Meat Promotion Executive),
New Zealand Lamb Information
Bureau, Reckitt & Colman Food
Division, Lea & Perrins, Olives from
Spain, Flour Advisory Bureau, British
Bacon Bureau, Home Baking Bureau,
Danish Agricultural Producers, The
Taunton Cider Co Ltd, The Honey
Bureau, The Pasta Information Center,
Colmans Foods, British Sausage Bureau*